ADVENT AND CHRISTMAS

WITH THE CHURCH FATHERS

ADVENT AND CHRISTMAS

WITH THE CHURCH FATHERS

A Seven-Week Retreat on the
Mystery and the Meaning of the Incarnation

TAN Books
Gastonia, North Carolina

Cover design by Jordan Avery

ISBN: 978-1-5051-3450-6
Kindle ISBN: 978-1-5051-3710-1
ePUB ISBN: 978-1-5051-3709-5

Published in the United States by
TAN Books
PO Box 269
Gastonia, NC 28053

www.TANBooks.com

Printed in India

The feast day of your birth resembles you, Lord,
because it brings joy to all humanity.
Old people and infants alike enjoy your day. Your day is celebrated from generation to generation. Kings and emperors may pass away, and the festivals to commemorate them soon lapse. But your festival will be remembered until the end of time.
Your day is a means and a pledge of peace.
At your birth heaven and earth were reconciled, since you came from heaven to earth on that day You forgave our sins and wiped away our guilt.
You gave us so many gifts on the day of your birth:
a treasure chest of spiritual medicines for the sick;
spiritual light for the blind;
the cup of salvation for the thirsty;
the bread of life for the hungry.
In the winter when trees are bare, you give us the most succulent spiritual fruit.
In the frost when the earth is barren, you bring new hope to our souls.
In December when seeds are hidden in the soil, the staff of life springs forth from the Virgin Womb.

Ephrem the Syrian (d. 373), The *Christmas Prayer*

O come, Redeemer of the earth, and manifest thy
virgin-birth.
Let every age in wonder fall: such birth befits the God
of all.
Begotten of no human will but of the Spirit,
Thou art still the Word of God in flesh arrayed, the
promised fruit to man displayed.
The Virgin's womb that burden gained, its virgin
honor still unstained.
The banners there of virtue glow; God in his temple
dwells below.
Proceeding from his chamber free that royal home of
purity a giant in twofold substance
one, rejoicing now his course to run.
O equal to the Father, thou! gird on thy fleshly mantle
now; the weakness of our mortal
state with deathless might invigorate.
Thy cradle here shall glitter bright, and darkness
breathe a newer light where endless
faith shall shine serene and twilight never intervene.
All praise, eternal Son, to thee, whose advent sets thy
people free, whom, with the
Father, we adore, and Holy Ghost, for evermore.
Amen.

St. Ambrose (d. 397), *Hymn on the Nativity of Christ*

Contents

Introduction

A Brief History of Christmas

At the end of every calendar year, from radios to retail, most of the world is caught up with the trappings of Christmas. Believers and Buddhists, Modernists and Muslims all seem to look forward to all the tinsel and the tunes December inevitably brings. City squares become bedecked, local shopping malls pipe in seasonal music, neighbors begin to decorate their front lawns and houses, yet it seems that devout Catholics are the only ones who actually know what Christmas is really about—Christ's Mass. Of course, the good cheer and extra acts of kindness are, for the most part, welcomed. But the heart of this season is the fact that the eternal and all-powerful Son of God draws near and takes on human flesh and blood. He lowers the heavens to be present visibly and truly to us on earth, and this is precisely what we celebrate at every Christ's Mass.

This do-it-at-home retreat is meant to take you through how the early Church Fathers thought, wrote, and preached about (what we call today) the four weeks of Advent, the Octave of Christmas (week 5), up through Epiphany (week 6), into the Baptism of the Lord, and its entrée into Ordinary Time (week 7). Here you will find theological reflections, prompts for your personal prayers, some questions for your own reflection, and prayers to guide you ever more deeply into the core mysteries of this time of year.

The oldest list of Christian martyrs we have is referred to as a book called the *Depositio Martyrum,* maybe best translated as *The Testimony of the Martyrs.* It was composed in 336, most likely by a secretary of Pope Damasus (d. 384). This work chronicles many of the better-known martyrs of Rome and beyond, providing the name, the day of the martyr's death, and—where possible—the location of his or her catacomb. The earliest names include the Apostles Paul and Peter, and from there Saints Perpetua and Felicity, brave martyrs in Carthage are mentioned (d. 202), Pope Callistus I (d. 222), with fifty-two martyrs being listed in all. Among this cataloging of those who paid the ultimate price for Christ are listed only two non-martyrial liturgical feasts: the feast of the Chair of St. Peter (February 22) and the Nativity of Our Lord on December 25.

As such, *The Testimony* stands as the earliest reference we have to a fixed date of December 25 prescribing when Christians are to celebrate Christmas. No reason for this date is provided; it is simply given. Such silence may, however, point to the fact that December 25 had been commemorated as Christmas for a very long time already. As early as 204, for example, Hippolytus of Rome had already accepted this date with convicted precision: "For the first advent of our Lord in the flesh, when he was born in Bethlehem, was December 25th, Wednesday, while Augustus was in his forty-second year, but from Adam, five thousand and five hundred years. He suffered in the thirty-third year, March 25th, Friday, the eighteenth year of Tiberius Caesar, while Rufus and Roubellion were Consuls."[1]

Many popular claims have argued that December 25 was chosen by the Christians in order to combat the popular Roman feast of the *Sol Invictus,* the Unconquerable Sun, marking the winter solstice, established by the pagan emperor Aurelian (270–75). While still an extremely widespread opinion, there is no real indication that Christmas was invented to rival a new imperial religious devotion. As the late Pope Benedict XVI put so succinctly

---

1 Hippolytus of Rome (d. c. 235), *Commentary on Daniel* 4.23.3; trans T. C. Schmidt, page 140, accessed here: https://www.pergrazia.com/wp-content/uploads/2019/12/0205_hippolytus_commentary-on-daniel_2010.pdf.

earlier, as the head of the Congregation for the Doctrine of the Faith, the first dating of Christmas was not "a Christian response to the cult of the unconquered sun promoted by Roman emperors in the third century in their efforts to establish a new imperial religion. . . . These old theories can no longer be sustained. The decisive factor was the connection of creation and Cross, of creation and Christ's conception."[2]

The truth is that we have been celebrating Christmas as we have for almost two thousand years, not because of December 25 but because of March 25. The December date was set not because of what non-Christians had been doing but because of what faithful Christians had already been believing. For most Christians celebrated March 25 as the day God originally created the universe, the day the Annunciation of the angel Gabriel to Mary occurred, and the first Good Friday when Christ Himself was crucified.

But why March 25? The early Christians naturally equated the spring equinox with the beginnings of the natural as well as the supernatural orders. The fresh newness of spring spoke to the early Christian writers about God's merciful entries into His own creation. For instance, Tertullian of Carthage (d. c. 240) held that Christ's crucifixion occurred "in the month of March, at the times of the Passover, on the eighth day before the calends of April, on the first day of unleavened bread, on which they slew the lamb at even, just as had been enjoined by Moses."[3] Bishop Augustine (d. 430) also held that Jesus Christ "is believed to have been conceived on 25 March, and also to have suffered that day."[4]

What is significant in this line of thought is that Jesus is now the calendar's creator. It is the Lord who orders time, with the pagan belief in astrology and fate coming to an end. In fact, Augustine

---

2 Joseph Cardinal Ratzinger, *The Spirit of the Liturgy* (San Francisco: Ignatius Press, 2000), 108.

3 Tertullian, Against the Jews §8; New Advent translation, https://www.newadvent.org/fathers/0308.htm.

4 St. Augustine, *On the Trinity*, Book 4.9, trans. Edmund Hill, *On the Trinity* (Hyde Park: New City Press, 1991), 159.

believed that the celebration of Christmas on December 25 was actually chosen by the Lord Himself. "Nor did he choose the day in the same way as people do, who vainly hang the fates of individuals on the dispositions of the stars. I mean, in this case the one who was born was not made lucky by the day, but he gave good luck to the day on which he was graciously pleased to be born."[5] There is something absolutely new and irrevocable with the God of the universe now being located in the womb of a virgin. This is it, a new age, the last age, the event that will mark all time.

Consequently, the importance of the Lord's birth also gave rise to other public manifestations of this Newborn's divinity. By the late fourth century, the feast of Epiphany was found throughout Christendom, signifying the entire world's recognition of this God-made-flesh. A century later, the first three public appearances of Christ's power came to be celebrated together—the Adoration of the Magi, the Baptism of Jesus by John in the Jordan, and the first open miracle of changing water into wine at the wedding feast in Cana. Peter, the great fifth-century bishop of Ravenna—known posthumously as "the Golden Mouthed," Peter Chrysologus (d. 450)—preached multiple sermons on why it is fitting these three manifestations be celebrated together:

> Although in the Mystery of the Lord's Incarnation itself there were clear signs of his eternal divinity, nevertheless today's feast discloses and reveals in manifold ways that God came into a human body, so that mortality, always enveloped in darkness, may not lose through ignorance what it has been made worthy of holding and possessing through such great grace.
>
> Today the wise man ponders with deep amazement what he sees and where: heaven on earth, earth in heaven; man in God, God in man; and the One who is not able to be contained in the whole world, he now sees confined in a tiny body. . . .
>
> Today Christ entered the River Jordan to wash away the sin of the world. John himself attests that he came for this

---

5 St. Augustine, *Sermon* 190.1, trans. Edmund Hill, *Sermons (184–229Z)* (New Rochelle, NY: New City Press, 1993), 38.

> reason: "Behold the Lamb of God, behold him who takes away the sin of the world" (Jn 1:29). Today the servant clings to his Lord, a man clings to God, John clings to Christ....
>
> Today Christ produces the first of his heavenly signs by changing water into wine, so that he whom the Father through his voice already pointed out as his Son would himself confirm that he was God through his miracles, because he who transforms the elements is the Author of the elements, and he who has no difficulty contravening nature has created nature himself....
>
> And so in these three ways the divinity of Christ has been indicated: by the Magi's offering, by the Father's testimony, and by the changing of the water into wine, since the authority of Scripture establishes that every word is confirmed by three verifications when it says, "Every word is confirmed by three witnesses" (Dt 19:15; Mt 18:16; 2 Cor 13:1). But because this feast itself urges us to come now to the Table of the Lord and to this chalice of gladness, let us be content to have confined such enormous matters within this brief sermon.[6]

With such an extended celebration of Christ's birth, with so many days and events to be commemorated, when does Christmas exactly end? We have the Advent preparation leading to Christmas itself (December 25), bringing us up to the Christmas Octave (January 1), which is not over until the twelve days of Christmas marked by the Epiphany (January 6), extending all the way to the feast of Candlemas (February 2). Various traditions and different times have called each of these "the end of Christmas," but our retreat will last seven weeks, up through Candlemas, the feast of the Presentation, and into the beginnings of Ordinary Time.

Liturgically, you will notice at your local parish, that the Christmas season ends with the celebration of the Baptism of the Lord. You will see how, on that Sunday, the priest is still draped in celebratory white, but on the very next day, green becomes the color of

---

6 St. Peter Chrysologus (d. 450), *Sermon* 160.1–7, trans. William Palardy, *St. Peter Chrysologus: Selected Sermons*, vol. 3 (Washington, DC: Catholic University of America Press, 2005), 277–81.

Monday's liturgy. Yet, although the Christmas season is officially over in today's United States, what some have called the Christmas Cycle does not end until forty days after the Birth of Jesus, February 2, and the feast of Candlemas.

Between the Epiphany and Candlemas, the Presentation of Our Lord, the Church eases back into *tempus per annum*, a time throughout the year which is commonly called "Ordinary Time." There are thirty-four weeks of "Ordinary Time" in the Church's liturgical year (broken up by Advent and Christmas and then by Lent and Easter) when our focus is to be turned toward how Jesus calls each of us into His intimate love and, consequently, into a missionary love for the world. For those four "ordinary" weeks between Epiphany and Candlemas, we shall hear the Gospels proclaim the presence and the power of Christ working miracles and slowly building up His Mystical Body. On February 2, the Church gathers to bless candles and to join Mary and Joseph in the presentation of their male son forty days after His birth. That is the cycle these weeks shall follow, so let us now look at how this do-it-at-home retreat suggests they be followed.

How to Approach These Pages

The entire liturgical year rightly begins with the season of Advent. This might be God's way of saying to us, "Good job this past year, but let's do it all over again." Advent is divided into four weeks corresponding to the themes of hope, peace, joy, and love. We should never tire of revisiting these essential gifts of the Christian life. Such reexamination is the only way for us mortals, who fall and fail so terribly often, to learn and grow in holiness. As a twentieth-century theologian and liturgist put it, because the Infinite One now meets us in the womb of His mother, bringing our littleness before His majesty is:

> in harmony with our human nature . . . [and that is why] the liturgical cycle is repeated year after year, just as the divine sacrifice is repeated in the Church day after day. As we are unable

> to exhaust our capacity for the Divine in a day or a year, the Church of Christ, with the infinite patience and the tender love of her divine Founder, continues to present to us the divine means of living Christ, thereby truly fulfilling her mission of achieving the ever increasing plenitude of the Redeemer. It is for this reason that the recurring daily and annual cycles of the liturgy never grow old for those who enter into their participation with the understanding and love of their divine Head. Ancient as the hills, the liturgy is still ever new, it has ever a new store of the divine life to hold out to our grasp, and with the recurring years the realization of its meaning grows ever richer.[7]

TAN is developing this series of do-it-at-home retreats in order to assist your participation in the life of the Church—her liturgies, sacraments, devotions, and teachings.

The following pages are divided into seven thematic chapters, following the seven weeks between Advent and Candlemas. Each week offers a focused collection of quotes from the Church Fathers, along with salient selections from the Bible, the Holy Mass, or the *Catechism of the Catholic Church* regarding the incarnation of the Son of God, His mother on earth, and all of us affected by this awe-filled event. Each week will also aim to center around the liturgy's Gospels proclaimed at Mass for that week's Sunday or feast day.

Your task in working your way through each week is to meditate slowly on whatever passage or word or image resonates within you. Read and meditate while always asking what the Spirit might be trying to teach you at any given moment. *Multum non multa,* "much of one thing and not many things," is a classic Latin adage to keep in mind. If you find yourself drawn to a particular passage or word, stay there and ask the Holy Spirit why this struck you so strongly. As you ponder these words, you might be drawn to write down what has resonated in your soul. To this end, along with each selection of text, you will also find space to answer some questions. Spend time

---

7 Virgil Michel, OSB (d. 1938), *The Liturgy of the Church: According to the Roman Rite,* 91–92.

looking at these questions and (knowing of course that you can do with these whatever you wish) asking the Holy Spirit to direct you toward the exercises that might produce the greatest fruit.

This ancient practice of reflecting on one's own life presupposes that God is working in your life in a way that He is not working in anyone else's life. You are His beloved, and His message to you conforms perfectly to your own personal state in life, your occupation, family situation, and all the other experiences that make up the unique story which is your life. Being as concrete as possible is the Christian's way of fighting against the convenient temptation of keeping God solely in the spiritual, reducing Him to an abstract being whose presence is necessary only in times of trial or, as in the minds of most today, only at the time of death, where it's my last chance to get it right. No, God is speaking to you now; He is speaking to you precisely as you are, right now. What follows is TAN Books' invitation to sit prayerfully with some of the most foundational Christian thinkers, to read their words, and then for you to invite the Holy Spirit to descend freshly into each moment in your life as you concretely show Him that you are now ready to grow in holiness.

The ultimate question to contemplate as you both begin and end this retreat is:

Do I desire to let Christ love me, to let Him into every aspect of my life, as He invites me to live His?

When a Christian explicitly sets time aside for daily prayer or an annual retreat, it is an ancient practice to begin each morning of your day by immediately turning your thoughts to the theme or the word or the special virtue the Lord might be speaking to you about that very day. As we begin this retreat, think about getting a journal—a pad of paper or simple notebook would do—and using this to record the messages and feelings that will no doubt come to you through the indwelling of the Holy Spirit. As in any relationship between persons, the more intentional and generous you are with the other (even God), the more He can be with you. Like anything, deepening our prayer life requires the execution of a definite plan, so do not be afraid to tell God what it is you want each day and exactly what gifts you hope to receive from Him.

While we can rest assured God will, in fact, do what He promises, we, too, must put into practice what we are now setting out to do. So, let's begin with some concrete particulars.

To begin, think about how true this is: You can only pray as you can, not as you can't. This axiom requires you to be honest with your own limitations and time commitments. You are (probably) not a monk or cloistered religious; you are (probably) a married person, maybe an extremely busy parent, someone living in the world of demands and deadlines, someone living out your God-given vocation in the messiness of the twenty-first century. That means you cannot pray as a desert hermit or a nun behind a grille; in fact, it would actually be sinful for you to try to find God outside the life He has given you. You are, therefore, to be "shrewd as serpents" (Mt 10:16) in figuring out how to let the Lord increase your holiness.

It is essential to remember that we cannot always control what comes in and out of our minds, but we can control our bodies. If you and the Lord determine that ten minutes, fifteen minutes, or a half hour (whatever it may be) is what you will commit yourself to, stay there for that ten minutes, that fifteen minutes, or that half hour—whatever you and the Holy Spirit have decided to do together. Even if you are drifting off to sleep, even if your mind is racing elsewhere, be still. Be still and gently ask the Lord to help bring your consciousness back to His presence within and before you. What you do not want to do is to think, "Oh well, nothing is happening; I'll come back later." Let's face it. You probably won't come back later because the kids will be home, you'll have to make supper, you'll be too tired, and so on. Commit yourself to a time and maybe even to a place and simply stay there. *That is your first and most fundamental commitment.*

Therefore, start by asking yourself and the Holy Spirit: How much time can we realistically devote to prayer each day? Be very truthful here: we rarely find the time; we must be intentional in carving out and making that time happen. What time of day is best for me to select that amount of time? Second: Where would I most in truth be able to do this—my bedroom, someplace in the house, in the car, at the office? In the end, begin with what is doable for you. Third: What do I truly want from this retreat? Where are my desires, my doubts, my fears, and my hopes? What do I want the Lord to know about me? What petition(s) do I want Him to hear and hopefully answer?

Ask the Holy Spirit to help you answer and commit to the following:

When you look ahead at the next seven weeks, how much time per day can you commit to meditating on these pages and giving yourself to private prayer?

I commit myself to __________ minutes of prayer each day, usually from _______ to ________, and, when possible, at this place:______________________.

Can you name what has motivated you to make this particular retreat at this time in your life?

Can you name the ways God might be speaking to you right now?

Who is Jesus for you? Do you talk to Him as a friend or as a judge? Have you ever asked Mary to let you hold the Christ Child? What image comes to mind when you think of Jesus gazing upon you?

We shall all, of course, have our own ideas swirling around these fundamental questions. We all have varied experiences of God's presence, and we are all unique and irreducible to anyone else. Your prayer life may look a lot like other Christians', but none of us will be identical in our desires and certainly not in our life's experiences. Nonetheless, God has each of us in mind as His beloved children and longs—yearns, even to the point of becoming one of us—to be more active in our lives.

Each of our seven weeks of retreat will begin with the theme for the Sunday Mass of that week. Between the First Sunday of Advent and the Presentation of our Lord, the Church works her way through the Old Testament prophecies of the Messiah's coming, the life of John the Baptist, and all the pivotal people involved at the birth of Christ—Mary, Joseph, the Wise Men, Anna and Simeon, and others. Every day's readings can be found on many websites (www.usccb.org, for example), and we encourage you to unite your retreat with the daily Mass readings. While the following is in no way a commentary on the Scriptures, all Christians must keep the Bible at the front and center of their prayer lives. This is the Word of God, the Word that points us to the Word, Jesus Christ. That is why Scripture and Sacred Tradition, as the two fonts of revelation, were given to us by Christ Himself. Keeping these two fonts together is your life as a Christian. It is for you that all of this was done, for your salvation and eternal joy. Consequently, be bold in bringing your daily experiences and fears and hopes and stresses to your prayer life and to the words that follow.

Some Preliminary Reflections

What memories or associations do I make with Advent and Christmas? Are these mainly positive and warm or sad and off-putting?

Has this season been more "commercial" or more spiritual for me so far in my life?

Have I ever tried to unite my prayer life more explicitly with this time of year?

What family traditions have I/we tried to foster for Advent and Christmas, if any?

What might I hope to see happen the next seven weeks? For my inner life? For those I love?

Am I willing to sacrifice some daily habits, and with that extra time, make space in this very busy time of the year to be more still, to listen, and to learn the value of waiting? What might I do practically to make this happen?

A Traditional Daily Advent Prayer

O Jesus, little child, come into my heart on Christmas morn, to wash away my sins and remain there in eternity. O Mary, Mother of my Savior, prepare for Jesus a cradle in my heart. Amen.

Nightly Marian Hymn During Advent and Christmas (Weeks 1–6)

Loving Mother of the Redeemer,
who remains the accessible Gateway of Heaven,
and Star of the Sea,
Give aid to a falling people
that strives to rise;
O Thou who begot thy holy Creator,
while all nature marvelled,
Virgin before and after
receiving that "Ave" from the mouth of Gabriel,
have mercy on sinners.

Alma Redemptóris Mater, quæ pérvia cæli
Porta manes, et stella maris, succúrre cadénti,
Súrgere qui curat pópulo: tu quæ genuísti,
Natúra miránte, tuum sanctum Genitórem
Virgo prius ac postérius, Gabriélis ab ore
Sumens illud Ave, peccatórum miserére

Week 1

The Hope of Advent

To be prayed from the first Sunday of Advent until Christmas Eve

℣. The Angel of the Lord brought tidings unto Mary
℟. And she conceived by the Holy Spirit.

Let us pray.

Pour forth we beseech Thee, O Lord, Thy grace into our hearts, that we to whom the Incarnation of Christ, Thy Son, was made known by the message of an Angel, may, by his Passion and Cross, be brought to the glory of his Resurrection. Through the same Christ, our Lord.
℟. Amen.

The term *Advent* is derived from two Latin terms: the prefix *ad-*, meaning toward, and the word *to come, venire,* which is a translation of the Greek *parousia,* meaning being (*ousia*) with (*para*), the term the New Testament employs for Christ's return at the end of time (e.g., Mt 24:27). The sense of Advent, or *parousia,* is that one arrives to a place or to a people in order to be purposefully among them. As such, it is a term that carries with it the sense of a deep presence. Advent, therefore, being the time the Church asks us to contemplate what it means that God Himself is now present to you—even more present than you are to yourself, as Augustine so wonderfully expressed it.[8]

As a liturgical season, Advent is first explicitly mentioned at the Synod of Saragossa in Spain in the year 380. In the next century, Pope Gelasius (d. 496) decreed that the five Sundays leading up to Christmas should prepare us for the birth of Christ, while Pope Gregory the Great (d. 604) provided the Church with the readings, prayers, and responses for those Sundays and the weeks in between. By the tenth century, Advent marks the beginning of a new liturgical year in the Church's calendar, and Pope Gregory VIII (d. 1085) finally sets Advent at four Sundays, determines the Octave of Christmas, the attendant feasts leading up to Epiphany, "ordinary time," and then the beginning of Lent.

On this First Sunday of Advent, one of the following Gospels will be proclaimed:

Mt 24:37–44 (Year A)
Mk 13:33–37 (Year B)
Lk 21:25–28, 34–36 (Year C)

What? Wait a second! None of these readings have to do with a sweet baby being born in a stable. They all have to do with the end of the world and a final judgment. Instead of a shining star, we get a darkening sun; instead of animals frolicking in the manger, we get animals fleeing onto the ark. What is going on?

Brace yourself; this is not a mistake. It is a reminder—the ultimate reminder—why the Lord comes to us in the first place. He comes to gather us all into His heavenly kingdom; He has come in order to save us from ourselves and the fallen world in which He has deigned to be born. "When the Church celebrates the *liturgy of Advent* each year, she makes present this ancient expectancy of

---

8 St. Augustine (d. 430), *Confessions* 3.6.11: "You were more intimately present to me than my innermost being, and higher than the highest peak of my spirit"; trans. Maria Boulding, *Confessions* (Hyde Park: New City Press, 1997), 83.

the Messiah, for in sharing in the long preparation for the Savior's first coming, the faithful renew their ardent desire for His second coming. By celebrating the precursor's birth and martyrdom, the Church unites herself to his desire: 'He must increase, but I must decrease.'"[9]

This looking ahead to the end of the world might surprise us, as we were simply looking forward to a comfortable few weeks before the joys of Christmas morning. But that is the point and paradox of this season—all children are born and only want to live and to make their way in this world, but the Christ Child has come into the world to die and be raised in order to thus open an entirely new world up to us. He comes first in simplicity in order to reign in splendor.

> We preach not one advent only of Christ, but a second also, far more glorious than the former. For the former gave a view of his patience; but the latter brings with it the crown of a divine kingdom. For all things, for the most part, are twofold in our Lord Jesus Christ: a twofold generation; one, of God, before the ages; and one, of a Virgin, at the close of the ages: his descents twofold; one, the unobserved, like rain on a fleece; and a second His open coming, which is to be. In his former advent, he was wrapped in swaddling clothes in the manger; in his second, he covers himself with light as with a garment. In his first coming, *he endured the Cross, despising shame* (Heb 12:2); in his second, he comes attended by a host of Angels, receiving glory. We rest not then upon his first advent only, but look also for his second. And as at his first coming we said, Blessed is he that comes in the Name of the Lord, so will we repeat the same at his second coming; that when with Angels we meet our Master, we may worship him and say, *Blessed is he that comes in the Name of the Lord*. The Savior comes, not to be judged again, but to judge them who judged him; he who before held his peace when judged, shall remind the transgressors who did those daring deeds at the Cross, and shall say, *These things have you done, and I kept silence*. Then, He came

9 *Catechism of the Catholic Church* §524 (hereafter, cited as CCC).

> because of a divine dispensation, teaching men with persuasion; but this time they will of necessity have him for their King, even though they wish it not.[10]

Cyril understands well the true nature of Christmas: it is not simply about fawning over the beauty of new life and cooing with a newborn babe—although it is that—but it is also about preparing for the end of the world and the final judgment of our own life stories. That is why the season of Advent is essential for the Christian. Advent is Jesus's way of asking us to prepare our hearts for what He has come into the world to achieve. This is not a one-day celebration but a lifelong training to live as we were all created to live—as saints!

While the preparations of Advent cannot help but be merry, have you begun also to notice the similarities between this season and the season of Lent? During these two liturgical times, the priest and the altar at Mass are draped in purple in order to signify a time of preparation and penance. Both seasons suppress the *Gloria*, waiting for Christmas Eve when the angels continue that hymn first heard above the birthplace of Jesus. Both seasons have a day of spiritual rest when we are commanded to "Rejoice" in anticipation the feast for which we are readying ourselves—*Laetare Sunday* in Lent and *Gaudete Sunday* in Advent.

Advent is thus a time of both preparation and penance. It is the quintessential Christian moment of "already but not yet." Like a mini-Lent and Easter, the movement of Advent-Christmas captures the best Catholic outlook on the world, knowing that the feasting is only truly joyful if preceded by the fasting. That is why the Church Fathers used this time of year to talk about the two comings of Christ—the one in time marked by the Lord's humility and simplicity, the other, still to come, which will be known by trumpet blasts and universal sovereignty. The first coming is that for

---

10 Cyril of Jerusalem, *Catechetical Lectures* 15.1 (preached c. 348); New Advent translation: https://www.newadvent.org/fathers/310115.htm. (slightly adjusted).

which we are now preparing, the second coming is that for which we should always be doing penance.

What does it mean for Jesus to come to me, to my family, this year?

Is there any one petition particularly pressing as I enter this Advent Season?

What area of my life is most in need of God's presence?

Do I truly desire to grow in Christian holiness? What would that even mean for me right now?

As you settle into Advent, the most immediate and recognizable symbol of this new season is the Advent wreath. This simple devotion is placed in the center of a table to remind us of the unquenchable love of Christ and to slowly await His visible appearance come Christmas. Think of the wreath. Its circular shape reminds us of how God's love is infinite, unbreakable, and unending; the evergreen pine branches speak to us of that same love being unfading and undying; and the candles are to speak to us of the Light who is Jesus, the One whose luster guides us on our way to heaven.

The four candles (usually three purple and one rose for *Gaudete Sunday*) teach us that Jesus Christ is "the light of God coming into the world" (cf. Jn 3:19) and how "darkness will not overpower him" (cf. Jn 1:5). These four candles, of course, represent the four weeks of Advent, but each has its own meaning as well. The first two weeks focus on Jesus's final coming as the just judge of the universe: the first candle is traditionally the candle of hope that the Lord is never far, while the second represents peace in both the world as well as in one's own heart. The second two weeks of Advent focus, first, on the gift of joy only Christ can bring; hence, the third candle is rose and lit on "Rejoice Sunday," while the fourth and final candle is for love. Many Advent wreaths also have a larger white candle placed directly in the middle of the wreath to be lit on Christmas and all during Christmastide as a symbol of Christ's new presence among us.

The medievals called hope "the virtue with wings" because it is the Holy Spirit's propelling us forward to things for which we can now only desire. Hope is the gift of the pilgrim, the empowerment to make one's way through arduous difficulties and remain buoyant in the face of obstacles. As with all the virtues, hope for the Christian is perfected by charity, realized only through serious prayer and joy. "Do not grow slack in zeal, be fervent in spirit, serve the Lord. Rejoice in hope, endure in affliction, persevere in prayer" (Rom 12:11–12).

When you were baptized, you received the three theological virtues of faith, hope, and love. How do you understand each of these gifts within you?

How might you explain how the Christian virtue of hope is different than the natural sense of optimism?

Pray over a time when Jesus Christ, as your hope, allowed you to persevere through a trial or very difficult time.

The Christian virtue of hope is inextricably tied to the other two theological virtues which were infused in you at baptism: faith and charity. Hope is more than optimism, therefore, just as faith is more than trust and charity more than kindness. Theological hope is, rather, a type of knowledge that what God has promised will for sure come true. Think of hope in this sense as your desire for things eternal—eternal love between you and God and friends (and eventually enemies!), eternal life, eternal joy and peace in heaven, and so on.

When we pray, one of the more comforting stories with which Jesus tries to win our trust is the story of the good and giving father who refuses to give his child anything harmful when asked for something good:

> And I tell you, ask and you will receive; seek and you will find; knock and the door will be opened to you. For everyone who asks, receives; and the one who seeks, finds; and to the one who knocks, the door will be opened. What father among you would hand his son a snake when he asks for a fish? Or hand him a scorpion when he asks for an egg? If you then, who are wicked, know how to give good gifts to your children, how much more will the Father in heaven give the Holy Spirit to those who ask him? (Lk 11:9–13)

Take some time to contemplate the key images of this reassuring encounter with Jesus:

1. The Father longs to open the door to eternity to you.
2. Would you ever harm another, especially one you love?
3. This is not pollyannish—Jesus knows you, "who are wicked," would never harm a child. How much more does God, who is perfect Love, desire to lavish His life upon you?

In the exceptional preaching abilities of St. Augustine of Hippo, this tale reflects the three theological virtues, with special attention paid to hope. Those in need ask for three things: bread and not a stone (cf. the story immediately preceding this one; Lk 11:5–8), fish and not a snake, and an egg instead of a scorpion. According to Augustine, bread is the sustenance of life, the symbol for charity which is ultimately what our existence is all about. Faith is like fish because it has to persevere through storms and the tempests of the times. "There remains hope, which as I see it can be compared to an egg," Augustine preaches. "Hope, you see, hasn't yet reached its object; an egg is something, but not yet a chick ... urging us to make light of the present and look to the future, forgetting what lies behind and stretching out to what lies ahead" (cf. Phil 3:13–14).

By associating hope with the future, Bishop Augustine then goes on to illumine his faithful by exhorting them not to dwell on their past. "So there is nothing so inimical to hope as looking backward.... But as long as the world is dripping with temptations, like the sulphureous rain of Sodom, we must be warned by the example of Lot's wife. She looked back, you see; and where she looked back, there was stuck."[11]

Does the evil spirit ever tempt you to stay stuck in the past?

How often do you beat yourselves up over past sins?

Do you really believe that it truly pleases God to hear from you and to answer your prayers?

---

[11] St. Augustine, *Sermon* 105.7 (preached 411); trans. Edmund Hill, *Sermons (94A–147A)* (Brooklyn: New City Press, 1992), 91.

Do you ever find yourself praying with a divided heart—that is, asking for things that you might want but know deep down are not of God?

What we are celebrating this week is the truth that this world is being redeemed not by power and might but by love and littleness. The Lord comes not as a savage warrior or an untouchable king, but as a baby, a son of Mary, the servant of the entire human race since the time of Adam. While never forfeiting His divinity, He chooses instead to come to us as one of us. Only God can save us, and only one like us can do that as one of us:

> The very Son of God, older than the ages, the invisible, the incomprehensible, the incorporeal, the beginning of beginning, the light of light, the fountain of life and immortality, the image of the archetype, the immovable seal, the perfect likeness, the definition and word of the Father: he it is who comes to his own image and takes our nature for the good of our nature, and unites himself to an intelligent soul for the good of my soul, to purify like by like. He takes to himself all that is human, except for sin. He was conceived by the Virgin Mary, who had been first prepared in soul and body by the Spirit; his coming to birth had to be treated with honor, virginity had to receive new honor. He comes forth as God, in the human nature he has taken, one being, made of two contrary elements, flesh and spirit. Spirit gave divinity, flesh received it.
>
> He who makes rich is made poor; he takes on the poverty of my flesh, that I may gain the riches of his divinity. He who is full is made empty; he is emptied for a brief space of his glory, that I may share in his fullness. What is this wealth of goodness? What is this mystery that surrounds me? I received the likeness of God, but failed to keep it. He takes on my flesh, to bring salvation to the image, immortality to the flesh. He

> enters into a second union with us, a union far more wonderful than the first.[12]

Here Gregory encapsulates the entire goal of Advent and Christmas: that God brings holiness to us as a man in order to make men and women holy. Purification can happen only "like by like." A poem of the early fifth century puts this beautiful theology into lovely images, contrasting what the Son of God is by nature and how He becomes the Son of Mary by choice, thus uniting His perfect godliness with our fallen humanness:

> In that virgin mother
> Human nature lost its primal stain and
> Power from above made flesh new.
> A maid unwed gave birth to God, Christ,
> Man from his Mother,
> God from his Father.
> From that day all flesh is divine,
> For flesh gave him birth and by this union
> Shares in God's nature.
> The word made flesh ceased not to be
> What he was before, though joined to flesh.
> Not made less by commerce with flesh
> His majesty lifts up unhappy men.
> What he always was he remains, and
> What he was not he begins to be.
> Now we are not what we were,
> But born to better things.
> He gives to me yet remains himself.
> By becoming what is ours God is not less,
> In giving us what is his he lifts us to heavenly gifts.[13]

---

12 St. Gregory of Nazianzen (d. 390), *Oration* 45; found in the *Liturgy of the Hours*, vol. I, Advent Season & Christmas Season (New York: Catholic Book Publishing Co., 1975), 161–62.

13 Prudentius (d. c. 410), *The Psychomachia* (*The Battle Within Our Soul*), lines 71–86; as in Robert Wilken, *The Spirit of Early Christian Thought* (New

The Old Testament reading this week asks us to consider how the Lord is drawing near. Jesus's presence come Christmas is what all the Old Testament writers yearned for. List three ways your life is different because Jesus Christ has been born into it.

What does it mean for you to invoke God as "Father"? Why do you think He chose to reveal Himself in this way to His chosen people? What images do you associate with the word father?

The Messiah knew only a desire for personal connection can move us toward our final end and ultimate purpose. Consider your own life: name what is most important to you, what moves you more than anything? Is it a "what" or a "who"? This is what Advent is trying to get us to see. Our hearts are made for more than "things," and authority and rules do not motivate us for very long.

Only a love that is personal, intimate, and eternal can fulfill what we have been made for—and that is why a personal, intimate, and eternal God becomes one with us, one for us, one *as* us. This is where we are to reorient our hope, in the person of a God-made-man. The early Church Fathers knew that if we placed our hope on anything else, on something temporal as if it were eternal—some thing or some mortal person as able to fulfill or complete us—it would only lead to despair.

In fact, that is what hell is portrayed to be: the loss of hope and the final settling for things we misused, things that should have led us to God but which instead became our god. When the great Italian poet Dante Alighieri (d. 1321) was looking for a slogan for hell, he thought there were no better words than, "Abandon hope, all ye

---

Haven: Yale University Press, 2003), 234.

who enter."[14] For the vice against hope is despair or despondency. This is more than just sorrow or having a "bad day." The vice of despair is when we lose trust in God's promise to redeem us and make us His own, often occurring when we think our sins and infidelities are more powerful than God's love and mercy. This is the vice of modern-day America. We live in a land full of opportunities but in a culture with values inverted: where wandering from place to place results in spiritual torpor, where myriad temptations keep us from committing to one life, one character, where we are rewarded for multitasking and valued for sacrificing depth and sincerity for speed and utility.

Consider the following quote from the *Catechism of the Catholic Church*. Ponder its words and ask yourself: (1) What in me still needs purification? (2) When and how do I become discouraged? What common patterns or themes can I trace through these times? (3) Does the thought of heaven really "buoy" me, or does it leave me either more sad or even indifferent? Why do I have this reaction?

> The virtue of hope responds to the aspiration to happiness which God has placed in the heart of every man; it takes up the hopes that inspire men's activities and purifies them so as to order them to the Kingdom of heaven; it keeps man from discouragement; it sustains him during times of abandonment; it opens up his heart in expectation of eternal beatitude. Buoyed up by hope, he is preserved from selfishness and led to the happiness that flows from charity.[15]

---

14 *Divine Comedy, Inferno,* Canto 3.9; trans. John Ciardi, *The Divine Comedy* (New York: New American Library, 1954), 32.

15 CCC §1818.

This is exactly why the author of the Letter to the Hebrews can be so bold, encouraging us to take refuge in God's truthfulness, trusting that the victory which is His will be fully ours as well one day:

> It was impossible for God to lie, we who have taken refuge might be strongly encouraged to hold fast to the hope that lies before us. This we have as an anchor of the soul, sure and firm, which reaches into the interior behind the veil, where Jesus has entered on our behalf as forerunner, becoming high priest forever according to the order of Melchizedek. (Heb 6:18–20)

The veil Jesus has entered is not simply the temple curtain but our human flesh. God has entered the human condition in order that we might be elevated to the divine condition. The Creator has become a creature because, as we have been focusing on, only "like" can purify "like." The remedy for our sickness cannot remain aloof but has to come to us, has to be close enough to make contact and so enter us.

The great physician Jesus Christ is not only the one who heals but also the one who is truly human. In our sinfulness, we are less than human—sometimes bordering on being truly beastly—and the Lord thus chooses to be born into our state in order to impart His own divine presence within each of us. That is the hope of Advent and the reality of Christmas.

> For just as the root of the vine ministers and distributes to the branches the enjoyment of its own and inherent natural quality, so the only-begotten Word of God, by putting his Spirit within them, imparts to the saints, as it were, a kinship to his own nature and the nature of God the Father, inasmuch as they have been united with him through faith and complete holiness of life; and he nourishes them to godliness, and works in them the knowledge of all virtue and well doing.[16]

---

16 Cyril of Alexandria (d. 444), *Commentary on John* 15.1, https://thedivinelamp.wordpress.com/2011/05/21/wednesday-may-25-st-cyril-of-alexandria-on-todays-gospel-john-151-8/.

> Jesus Christ is a great medicine. If this medicine can't cure pride, I don't know what will. He's God, and he becomes man; he lays aside his divinity; that is, he is sort of puts it in a safe deposit; that is to say, he hides what was his very own, and appears openly in what he had taken on. He becomes a human being, though he is God; and we human beings don't admit to being human, that is, we don't acknowledge we are mortal, we don't admit we are fragile, we don't admit we are sinners, we don't acknowledge we are sick, and so at least, being sick, go looking for a doctor. What is much more dangerous, we imagine we are perfectly well![17]

The parable of the vine and the branches in John 15 is a provocative image for the Christian life. The vine is the source of all the nutrients, the stability, and the fruitfulness of the branches which spring forth from it. In our search for piety, we probably tend to concentrate on Christ as the vine and forget the other half of this parable. Of course, the vine is necessary: it is that part of a plant that is the support and the strength of everything else. Yet as necessary as that branch is to the rest of the plant, that vine also needs those branches in order to bear fruit. Without a branch or offshoot, a vine remains dormant and eventually decays. The branches carry the life of the vine into the world in multiple and varied ways, extending the vine into places it could never otherwise reach.

Christ has chosen you to continue His birth into this world. You are His advent in a mystical sense—the one in whom He wills His presence to be extended. Reflect on the passages above and ask yourself:

Am I a faithful branch in the Lord's garden? What is the fruit I bear?

---

17 St. Augustine, *Sermon* 77.11; trans. Edmund Hill, *Sermons (51–94)* (Brooklyn, NY: New City Press, 1991), 322–23.

Do I ever imagine myself as an extension of the Lord's own presence, His own advent?

Where do I think I need the most pruning in order to be the most fruitful? (cf. Jn 15:1–2)

Do I really believe that the Spirit of Jesus Christ is already within me? What might I need to do to recover that "godliness" deep within my soul?

The parable of the vine and the branches is the biblical basis for the Catholic understanding of the Mystical Body. Christ has come not simply to be adored but has come to create this incredible interconnectedness—interconnection between God and man and between angels and men, and between all persons across the globe as well as across all time.

> The Church is like a human being. For soul it has the sanctuary, for mind the divine altar, for body the nave. The Church is the image and likeness of the human being who himself has been created in the image and likeness of God. By its nave, as by the body, it enables the gaining of practical wisdom; by its sanctuary, as by the soul, it gives a spiritual interpretation of the contemplation of nature; by the divine altar, as by the mind, it reaches the vision of God. Conversely, the human being is a mystical church. By the nave of his body he enlightens his active powers . . . by the sanctuary of his soul he offers to God the spiritual essences of things . . . by the altar of his mind he invokes the silence in the heart of the divine word, with a

> loud voice that surpasses all knowledge. There, as far as is allowed to humanity, he is united to the godhead . . . and receives the imprint of its dazzling splendor.[18]

Often, when Catholics think of "the Church," what comes to mind are only the professionally religious—the pope, the bishops, one's local priest and pastor, and perhaps a habited sister or two. As necessary as these offices are, the Church is ultimately Christ alive in you right now. The Church is neither a building nor is it a reality reserved for some. The Church exists wherever one assents to Jesus as ultimate Lord. That is why the Greek and Latin for "Church" is *ecclesia,* a word meaning to be called (*kaleo-*) out (*ex-*) of the world and into the divine life.

This "call" is not just an impromptu nudge. In the Bible, this is the word used when Moses is called nearer the burning bush (cf. Ex 3), what awakens Samuel as the Lord rouses him from sleep deep within the Temple (cf. 1 Sm 3). It is the word used for a divine purpose and plan for one's life. You too have been called to own this truth as well: like the better-known heroes of the Christian story, you too have a place and a role to fulfill. It might be husband or wife, mother or father, son or daughter, friend, colleague, community member, and so on—and that is what Advent is preparing us to see.

Perhaps Advent is *the* Christian time for paradox: the Church's way of preparing us to see how a God who cannot be contained by the heavens is now securely safe in His mother's womb, how the sting of death will be remedied through the vulnerability of a newborn, how the Omnipotent will reveal Himself simply to melt our hearts and hope we fall in love with Him. At the heart of this love affair stands Mother Mary and her immaculate *fiat,* that graced "let it be done" however the Father wills to save His good creation.

---

18 Maximus the Confessor, *Mystagogia* §6; trans. Olivier Clément, *The Roots of Christian Mysticism* (Hyde Park: New City Press, 1995), 126. A "confessor" is one who dies at a later date due to wounds incurred for the faith but having survived his original torture and is not technically invoked as a "martyr." We shall rely on Clément's anthology throughout, as it contains illuminating and lengthy excerpts from the Church Fathers.

Blessed is she: she has received the Spirit who made her immaculate.
She has become the temple in which dwells the Son of the heights of heaven. . . .
Blessed is she: through her the race of Adam has been restored, and those who had deserted the Father's house have been brought back. . . .
Blessed is she: within the bounds of her body was contained the Boundless One who fills the heavens, which cannot contain him.
Blessed is she: in giving our life to the common Ancestor, the Father of Adam, she renewed fallen creatures.
Blessed is she: she gave her womb to him who lets loose the waves of the sea.
Blessed is she: she has born the mighty giant who sustains the world, she has embraced him and covered him with kisses.
Blessed is she: she has raised up for the prisoners a deliverer who overcame their jailer.
Blessed is she: her lips have touched him whose blazing made angels of fire recoil.
Blessed is she: she has fed with her milk him who gives life to the whole world.
Blessed is she: for to her Son the saints all owe their happiness.
Blessed be the Holy One of God who has sprung from thee.[19]

Seeing how God surprises us in this season, choosing a nine-month gestation and being born of a woman, rather than some sort of clean airdrop from heaven, He knows we have to prepare ourselves to receive Him as He chooses to come to us and not as

---

19 Jacob of Sarugh (d. 521), *Hymn to the Mother of God*; trans. Clément, *The Roots of Christian Mysticism*, 42. Along with Ephrem the Syrian (d. 373) and a monk known simply as Narsai (d. 502), Jacob is one of great poet-theologians of Christian Syria.

we think God has to act. How often the Lord will speak to you in the car and not necessarily in Church; how His love will strike you deeply as you gaze upon your beloved spouse, child, or friend, perhaps even more than when gazing upon a religious picture, and so on. Christianity is truly the religion of the everyday.

> It happens at certain moments that delight and enjoyment invade the whole body. And the fleshly tongue can say no more; to such a degree now have earthly objects become but dust and ashes. The initial delights, those of the heart, fill us while we are awake. The spirit burns at the hour of prayer, at the moment of reading, in the course of frequent meditations or long contemplations. But the final delights come to us differently, often during the night, in the following way: when we are between sleep and wakefulness, when we are asleep without being asleep and awake without being really awake. These delights invade a person and the whole body throbs. It is clear then that this is nothing other than the kingdom of heaven.[20]

Another paradox: the kingdom of God is not something we observe but something we experience and thus become. It is that sense of the divine indwelling of which we get a sense every now and then. Perhaps it is during a spiritual practice like Eucharistic Adoration or during absolution in the sacrament of Reconciliation, but—as Isaac knows—it could also come while reading or at night, as we are in that space between sleep and being awake. The Lord chooses when and how to meet us, not the other way around. Those whose preconceived categories and doctrinal boxes are clear and tidy (which usually means rigid as well) can easily miss how the Christ Child is looking to come to them.

That is why the first week of Advent exhorts all to "stay awake," to be watchful, because we do not know what the next moment of our lives brings—it may very well be the last moment. Jesus, therefore, asks us all to live in a state of constant vigilance. We can do

---

20 Isaac of Nineveh (d. c. 700), *Ascetic Treatises* §8; Clément, *The Roots of Christian Mysticism*, 254.

this, as Paul teaches, by "praying always" (1 Thess 5:17), and we do this by fostering an internal sense of gratitude for every one of these fleeting but so beautiful moments of life. We "search" for Christ by being constantly aware that every moment is His gift to us—every morning and noon, every evening and night, all those in our lives, and all that He has asked us to do and to receive. In this constant state of gratitude for the fragility of human existence, do we learn to "savor" every gift from God.

Of course, there are different reasons to stay awake. Whatever those might be, pray to convert any sleeplessness these days into a prayerful vigilance, awaiting the Lord's return as you lie in the dark hours of early morning, contemplating all the blessings which are yours.

> Joyous (cf. Dan 4:13) were today the Watchers, that the Wakeful came to wake us! Who would pass this night in slumber, in which all the world was watching? Since Adam brought into the world the sleep of death by sins, the Wakeful came down that He might awake us from the deep sleep of sin. Watch not we as usurers, who thinking on money put to interest, watch at night so oft, to reckon up their capital, and interest. Wakeful and cautious is the thief, who in the earth has buried and concealed his sleep. His wakefulness all [comes to] this, that he may cause much wakefulness to them that be asleep. Wakeful likewise is the glutton, who has eaten much and is restless; his watching is to him his torment, because he was impatient of stint. Wakeful likewise is the merchant; of a night he works his fingers telling over what pounds are coming, and if his wealth doubles or trebles. Wakeful likewise is the rich man, whose sleep his riches chase away: his dogs sleep; he guards his treasures from the thieves. Wakeful also is the careful, by his care his sleep is swallowed: though his end stands by his pillow, yet he wakes with cares for years to come. Satan teaches, O my brethren, one watching instead of another; to good deeds to be sleepy, and to ill awake and watchful. Even Judas Iscariot, for the whole night through was wakeful; and he sold the righteous Blood, that purchased the whole world. The son of

> the dark one put on darkness, having stripped the Light from off him: and Him who created silver, for silver the thief sold. Yea, Pharisees, the dark one's sons, all the night through kept awake: the dark ones watched that they might veil the Light which is unlimited. You then watch as [heaven's] lights in this night of starry light. For though so dark be its color yet in virtue it is clear.[21]

Where do you feel vigilant, and where do you feel drowsy in your spiritual life?

Are you awake at night when you would rather be asleep? How do you use that precious time?

Do you long for the kingdom of Christ?

Do you live in the truth that we are in the final days?

What might you need to prepare for your last night or day on earth? Be specific.

---

[21] Ephrem the Syrian (d. 373), *Hymn on the Nativity* 1; New Advent translation: https://www.newadvent.org/fathers/3703.htm.

This first week of Advent has stressed Christ's coming in Bethlehem alongside His coming at the end of time. But might we not also talk about a third coming? Of course, God has come in the flesh and has changed the course of human history for all time; and, yes, the Messiah will come again at a time and place we might most likely miss, and that is why the first Sunday of Advent always exhorts us to "stay awake," to be vigilant, and ready to receive the Lord.

But does He not also come at this very moment? The signs and smells, the bells and all the bows, the carols and the cookies of Advent will no doubt bring the Lord close to our minds and hearts, if not all our senses. This third coming is mystical and sacramental but no less real than Jesus's coming before in Bethlehem or will absolutely at the Final Judgment. These pages have been compiled to help you prepare for this third coming, this breaking in of grace into your soul here and now.

This is what all those in the Old Testament longed to experience, and the Lord knew: "But blessed are your eyes, because they see, and your ears, because they hear. Amen, I say to you, many prophets and righteous people longed to see what you see but did not see it, and to hear what you hear but did not hear it" (Mt 13:16–17). God-made-man, the Word-made-flesh, the union of heaven and earth, of Creator and creation—this is what the human heart was made to encounter, made to partake of such a wedding feast!

> Wherefore also the Lord Himself gave us a sign, in the depth below, and in the height above, which man did not ask for, because he never expected that a virgin could conceive, or that it was possible that one remaining a virgin could bring forth a son, and that what was thus born should be God with us, and descend to those things which are of the earth beneath, seeking the sheep which had perished, which was indeed His own peculiar handiwork, and ascend to the height above, offering and commending to His Father that human nature which had been found, making in His own person the first-fruits of the resurrection of man; that, as the Head rose from the dead, so also the remaining part of the body—namely, the body of everyman who is found in life—when the time is fulfilled of that

> condemnation which existed by reason of disobedience, may arise, blended together and strengthened through means of joints and bands (cf. Eph 4:16) by the increase of God, each of the members having its own proper and fit position in the body. For there are many mansions in the Father's house (cf. Jn 14:2), inasmuch as there are also many members in the body.[22]

The anguished cry of the lonely, the screams of the wounded, the tears of the betrayed all find a remedy here. That is how we can see our own history in the history of Israel: we too have been created for covenant, we too have hardened our hearts against God's gentle invitations, we too have been chastised, and we too can turn back anytime we are humble enough to do so.

And how does healing come to humanity? Lists of instructions and all the rules in the world simply do not work. We are not healed by the law; we are not saved from anything external to us. How could we be? The medicine has to be swallowed, the injection has to pierce the skin. The corruption is internal, so the cure must be as well. We have gone wrong not just in what we do but in who we have become—a race foreign to who we were meant to be. The solution then has to be something other than words, something other than an intellectual program. It has to be personal, and it has to be intimate, so close we become one with it. That is why we await a God to be made man, one who is so perfect He can actually heal, but one who is so close He actually can work from within each of us personally and privately.

> And the Creator saw that their wound was grown great, and needed the care of a physician—and Jesus Himself is their Creator, and Himself heals them—and He sent forerunners before His face. And we are not afraid to say of Moses the Lawgiver that he is one of His forerunners, and that the same Spirit which was with Moses worked also in the choir of the saints; and they all prayed for the Only-begotten Son of God.

[22] Irenaeus of Lyons (d. c. 202), *Against Heresies*, III, 19.3; New Advent translation: https://www.newadvent.org/fathers/0103319.htm.

> John again is one of His forerunners: and for this cause the Law and the Prophets were until John, and 'the kingdom of God suffereth violence, and the violent take it by force.' (Mt 11:12–13) And being clothed with the Spirit, they saw that none among the creatures was able to heal that great wound, but only the bounty of God, that is to say His Only-begotten, whom He sent to be the Savior of all the world; for He is the great physician, who is able to heal the great wound. And they asked God, and of His bounty the Father of creatures spared not His Only-begotten for our salvation, but delivered Him up for us all and for our iniquities. (Rom 8:32) And He humbled himself, and by his stripes we all were healed. (Phil 2:8, Is 53:5) And by the word of His power He gathered us out of all lands, from one end of the world to the other end of the world, and raised up our hearts from the earth, and taught us that we are members one of another.[23]

What a lovely image for this first week of Advent! Men as holy as Moses attempted to build a house for God to dwell in. He wanted the wounds of his people healed, and so he received the Law and transmitted it to those in his care. Yet those wounds continued to fester, sin still reigned. The infirmity could be remedied only by one who was by nature not infirmed, so God comes to His people, the True Physician to the infirmed, Bethlehem being the ultimate house call! For our sake, the doctor becomes sick, the innocent sheep is led to the slaughter, God is crucified.

Continuing to focus on the gift of hope, let us pray through a fifth-century litany to the way faith and hope lead to love and joy, transforming us into the one on whom we long to gaze—Christ Himself.

> First definition: faith. A thought about God free of idolatry.
>
> Second definition: hope. A loving pilgrimage of the spirit

[23] St. Antony the Great (d. 356), *epistle* 3; accessed at: https://www.johnsanidopoulos.com/2018/01/the-seven-great-letters-of-saint_19.html#:~:text=Truly%20my%20beloved%20in%20the,He%20makes%20for%20His%20creatures.

towards what is hoped for.

Third definition: patience. Ceaseless perseverance in seeing with the inner eye the Invisible as if it were visible.

Fourth definition: absence of avarice. To be as eager not to possess as people usually are to possess.

Fifth definition: knowledge. To disregard oneself in the effort to ascend to God.

Sixth definition: humility. Never thinking about what one deserves.

Seventh definition: absence of irascibility. The ability to avoid anger.

Eighth definition: integrity (or interior chastity). The inward sense constantly united to God.

Ninth definition: love. An increased friendliness towards those who insult us.

Tenth definition: total transformation.

In the enjoyment of God the anguish of death becomes joy.[24]

As your retreat continues, keep this in mind: the goal of the Christian life is not to follow the rules or to be able to quote the Scriptures or holy words of the Faith. The goal of the Christian life is union with Christ and our becoming more and more like Him. It is a "total transformation" of the human intellect, will, and all our bodily acts. It is in how we think and feel, in how we speak, and in how we conduct our lives.

What might conversion of heart mean for you?

What worked for you this week, and what might you change in week 2?

24 Diadochus of Photike (d. c. 500), *Gnostic Chapters, Preamble*; Clément, *The Roots of Christian Mysticism*, 139–40.

What were the greatest graces of this past week? Pray over those gifts and ask God why they are staying with you so powerfully.

As you work your way through this retreat at this very special time of the year, we are encouraging you to pay attention to the readings of Advent and Christmas. The Church provides the entire story of salvation history during the liturgical year through the readings from the Old Testament, the proclamation of the Psalms, from the New Testament Epistles and, of course, the daily Gospel. But there is another source of prayer you can use as well—the parts of the Mass.

Too many Catholics forget that the prayers of the Mass situate us in a particular movement of the liturgical year and therefore capture what it is the Church is especially celebrating at that time. In Advent, there are two Prefaces, the part of the Mass between the faithful's first standing after the priest washes his hands and before the Sanctus. Preface I of Advent has the Church praying in these words:

> It is truly right and just, our duty and our salvation, always and everywhere to give you thanks, Lord, holy Father, almighty and eternal God, through Christ our Lord.
>
> For he assumed at his first coming the lowliness of human flesh, and so fulfilled the design you formed long ago, and opened for us the way to eternal salvation, that, when he comes again in glory and majesty and all is at last made manifest, we who watch for that day may inherit the great promise in which now we dare to hope.
>
> And so, with Angels and Archangels, with Thrones and Dominions, and with all the hosts and Powers of heaven, we sing the hymn of your glory. Holy, Holy, Holy . . .

Do you ever pray over the Mass prayers? These are easy to find online and can enhance your active participation in the Holy Sacrifice.

St. Jerome famously said in his introduction to the *Commentary on Isaiah*, "Ignorance of scripture is ignorance of Christ." Do you take time to pray over the readings for Mass? Have you ever felt inspired to spend prayer time simply reading through the Bible, or at least manageable books of the Old Testament, the Psalms, the Gospels, or the New Testament letters?

When we come to see how widespread Christmas cheer is meant to be, we might finally give Advent its proper due and not rush our Lord's birth. Advent is intended to be a time of prayer and penitential preparation, not filled with festive office parties as commercialism has made it. If it's possibly too late, think about this for next year: you might intentionally search out Advent music instead of Christmas carols, you might wait until Christmas Eve to put the Christ Child in the creche, or you might even make the daily Advent calendar a time of family prayer and reflection. Once Christmas is seen as more than a morning of frantic revelry, perhaps Advent can recover its own time and tone as well.

The season of Advent is meant to ready us to better deepen our awareness of the implications of God's becoming flesh, and this is where "the world" actually gets a few things right when it comes to the mystery of God's incarnation. Inevitably catching something from the true meaning of Christmas, secular society bombards our senses with bright lights and carols, with the smells and tastes of cookies and various dishes, and all the other ways Jesus's coming shines through even those who are not conscious of His presence. But this makes sense: because God has taken on matter, all matter is now able to be the lens through which we meet the divine. Think of how the radio stations change their formats for a few weeks in December, how the public square has been decorated, and how all the new lights around town have the potential of lifting our eyes and ears to the One in whose image and likeness we have all been created.

> Our whole nature had to be recalled from death to life. God therefore stooped over our dead body to offer his hand, so to speak, to the creature lying there. He came near enough to death to make contact with our mortal remains, and by means of his own body provided nature with the capacity for resurrection, thus by his power raising to life the whole of humanity. . . . In our body the activity of any one of our senses communicates sensation to the whole of the organism joined to that member. It is the same for humanity as a whole, which forms, so to speak, a single living being: the resurrection of one member extends to all, and that of a part to the whole, by virtue of the cohesion and unity of human nature.[25]

The mystical theologian Gregory of Nyssa here likens Christ's coming into time to one of our senses affecting our entire body. Think of how a sweet smell can invoke memories or a familiar sight from long ago can soothe your nostalgic heart. Analogously, when the Son of God takes to Himself our human nature, this one act affects the entire human race. It also affects the entire created order now that God has become part of His own good creation.

That is how Christmas is a most Christian event—all matter becomes consecrated once God Himself is born. God Himself is now taking milk, dressed in swaddling clothes, breathing our air and seeing our world, reaching out to others, to animals, to the

---

[25] Gregory of Nyssa, *Catechetical Oration* 32; Clément, *The Roots of Christian Mysticism*, 46–47.

earth, and so on. It is in this way that it is right to decorate our trees, and to bring in lights, and to bake new foods, and to sing new songs.

Yet, still being the season of Advent, could you think about not jumping right into Christmas carols but looking up songs more appropriate for these four weeks of preparation? Perhaps you could find these, as a few examples:

- *O Come, O Come, Emmanuel*: originally from the late eighth or early ninth century, this Latin chant prepares us for the coming of Christ by invoking the ancient Messianic titles for Jesus, the seven "O Antiphons" which (as you will see) the Church will use beginning December 17 each year.
- *Wachet auf! ruft uns die Stimme*: first appearing in 1599 in the German Lutheran community, J. S. Bach (d. 1750) popularized this call to be vigilant and ready when the Lord at last appears, thus often known by its English, "Sleepers, Awake."
- *Of the Father's Heart Begotten* or *Of the Father's Love Begotten*: based on a fifth-century hymn by Aurelius Prudentius (d. 413), *Corde Natus*, this may be one of the oldest Christian songs still sung today, teaching us how the chaos of the fallen world is surrounded and eventually sanctified by God's indefatigable love for us.
- *Gabriel's Message* or *The Angel Gabriel from Heaven Came*: rooted in Luke 1:26–28, coming into English as a folk carol most popular in the Basque region of Spain, is originally from a fourteenth-century hymn focusing our thoughts on that timeless encounter between the angel Gabriel and Mother Mary.
- *Es ist ein Ros' entsprungen*: German for "A Rose has sprung up," is poetically referring to the Blessed Virgin as the Rose of the human race, springing up from her Immaculate

Conception to give the world the birth of her saving Son.

- *On Jordan's Bank*: composed by the rector of the University of Paris, Charles Coffin (d. 1749), a rigorist follower of the strict theology of Jansenism, this hymn reminds us of John the Baptist's central role in Advent, preparing the way for Jesus to enter our hearts.
- *Come, Thou Long Expected Jesus*: from the founder of Methodism, Charles Wesley (d. 1788), this Advent hymn aims to whet our expectation for the Lord's visible appearance on Christmas, Wesley wrote that he based his words on the Old Testament prophet Haggai: "I will shake all the nations, so that the treasures of all the nations will come in. And I will fill this house with glory—says the Lord of hosts" (Hag 2:7).
- *The King of Glory Comes, the Nation Rejoices*: a priest for the Archdiocese of Chicago, W. F. Jabusch (d. 2018) composed this hymn in the late '60s after he visited the Holy Land, basing the song on an Jewish folk song he heard while in Israel.

Besides whirling in our ears, Christmas must also impress upon our eyes, and the most common visuals this time of year are, of course, the creche and the Christmas tree. Be sure not to place the baby Jesus in the creche before Christmas, and do pay attention to when you bring in the Magi, the three Wise Men appearing only after the birth of Christ. There is no Church Father who attests to anything like a creche, but we can look much later to St. Francis of Assisi (d. 1274) to find its humble beginnings. Francis's biographer, Thomas de Celano, tells us this:

> It should be recorded and held in reverent memory what Blessed Francis did near the town of Greccio (in Italy), on the feast day of the Nativity of our Lord Jesus Christ, three years before his glorious death. In that town lived a certain man by

> the name of John who stood in high esteem, and whose life was even better than his reputation. . . . Blessed Francis often saw this man. He now called him about two weeks before Christmas and said to him: "If you desire that we should celebrate this year's Christmas together at Greccio, go quickly and prepare what I tell you; for I want to enact the memory of the Infant who was born at Bethlehem and how He was deprived of all the comforts babies enjoy; how He was bedded in the manger on hay between an ass and an ox. For once I want to see all this with my own eyes." When that good and faithful man had heard this, he departed quickly and prepared in the above-mentioned place everything that the Saint had told him. . . . Greccio became a new Bethlehem. The night was made radiant like the day, filling men and animals with joy. The crowds drew near and rejoiced in the novelty of the celebration. Their voices resounded from the woods, and the rocky cliffs echoed the jubilant outburst. As they sang in praise of God the whole night rang with exultation. The Saint of God stood before the crib, overcome with devotion and wondrous joy. A solemn Mass was sung at the crib. The Saint, dressed in deacon's vestments, for a deacon he was, sang the Gospel. Then he preached a delightful sermon to the people who stood around him, speaking about the nativity of the poor King and the humble town of Bethlehem. . . . And whenever he mentioned the Child of Bethlehem or the Name of Jesus, he seemed to lick his lips as if he would happily taste and swallow the sweetness of that word.[26]

Once again, it is the Christian saint who gives us so much of our cultural heritage, a heritage whose roots are forgotten or ignored by the many today. St. Francis's presepio was a way of reenacting the first Christmas, inviting people to imagine themselves before the Holy Family and to offer whatever devotion would well up in their hearts. Could you make your manger scene somehow a place for

---

[26] Thomas de Celano, *The First Life of St. Francis*, ch. 30; accessed at https://dmdhist.sitehost.iu.edu/francis.htm.

prayer, perhaps with a suitable chair or with fitting reading material nearby?

Regarding a more Christian approach to the family Christmas tree, consider using the first Sunday of Advent to get the tree in and up at your house. Such a tradition arose relatively late in Christianity, originating across Germany and today's Baltic States sometime in sixteenth-century Lutheranism. Here, the evergreen is to evoke feelings of eternity, the lights, of course, remind us of the illuminating presence of Jesus in our minds and lives, while the ornaments are usually figurines commemorating some religious event or stirring up some joyful memory, such as a family picture or well-known Christmas symbol or figure. The angel on top of the tree is to remind us of Gabriel, whom God sent to begin this epic journey, or the star who led the nations on their own journey to the Christ Child.

While all of this can involve much work, try to place it in prayer—perhaps beginning the house's decorating with a decade of the Rosary, using the Annunciation of the Joyful Mysteries. Also, try to remember that all of this labor is not how we win God's closeness, but is how we simply open up our homes and hearts to receive Him in a childlike wonder. So, lest we limit our imagining Advent as our searching for God, we should be careful to keep in mind that this season is really about God's search for us. Out of love for a forlorn people, He leaps down from heaven. He comes yet again this year (and, in fact, again at every moment we allow Him), and these four weeks are about settling our heart in patient hope and in joyful love so we can receive Him as much as personally possible this year.

Extended Prayer Period: One of the more poignant stories of God's search for us is Jesus's encounter with Zacchaeus in Luke 19.

> Jesus came to Jericho and intended to pass through the town. Now a man there named Zacchaeus, who was a chief tax collector and also a wealthy man, was seeking to see who Jesus was; but he could not see him because of the crowd, for he was short in stature. So he ran ahead and climbed a sycamore tree in order to see Jesus, who was about to pass that way. When he

reached the place, Jesus looked up and said to him, "Zacchaeus, come down quickly, for today I must stay at your house." And he came down quickly and received him with joy. When they all saw this, they began to grumble, saying, "He has gone to stay at the house of a sinner." But Zacchaeus stood there and said to the Lord, "Behold, half of my possessions, Lord, I shall give to the poor, and if I have extorted anything from anyone I shall repay it four times over." And Jesus said to him, "Today salvation has come to this house because this man too is a descendant of Abraham. For the Son of Man has come to seek and to save what was lost" (Lk 19:1–10).

Read through this encounter with Jesus a couple of times. Close your eyes and imagine this scene unfolding in your life. Where are you? What feelings surface when you hear Jesus is coming nearer and nearer. What limitations (like Zacchaeus's shortness) must you overcome in order to see Jesus, in order for Him to see you? How do you feel when He calls you by name and invites you closer, begging to stay in your home this day—in your home, your heart, your life? Like Zacchaeus, do you ever try to barter or win over Christ's love, promising Him things and trying to impress Him ("I shall give to the poor . . .")? Are you able to sit simply in His undeserved, unmerited love and just see His eyes and hear His words, "Today salvation has come to you"?

Grant your faithful, we pray, almighty God, the resolve to run forth to meet your Christ with righteous deeds at his coming, so that, gathered at his right hand, they may be worthy to possess the heavenly kingdom. Through our Lord Jesus Christ, your Son, who lives and reigns with you in the unity of the Holy Spirit, God, for ever and ever.

Week 2

The Peace of Advent

To be prayed from the first Sunday of Advent until Christmas Eve

℣. The Angel of the Lord brought tidings unto Mary
℟. And she conceived by the Holy Spirit.

Let us pray.

Pour forth we beseech Thee, O Lord, Thy grace into our hearts, that we to whom the Incarnation of Christ, Thy Son, was made known by the message of an Angel, may, by his Passion and Cross, be brought to the glory of his Resurrection. Through the same Christ, our Lord.
℟. Amen.

The readings for the second week of Advent speak to us of our need for repentance and conversion of heart. The world certainly does not recognize this aspect of Advent, but this call to contrition is what makes Christianity so beautiful and its view of the human person so dignified. Think of it: even God Himself will not come to us if we do not want Him. Love respects; love never forces; love rarely demands. Jesus Christ comes to each of us in humility in the hope that each heart will freely receive Him. In this way, each and every human person gets what he or she desires: if our "no" remains persistent and lifelong, we get what we deserve and are free to spend eternity as we wish; if we utter even the faintest "yes"—however desperate—we get what God wants and what we were made for: unending happiness.

This ultimate decision is not something reserved for only some future moment. It begins now. In fact, it begins afresh with every new liturgical year that Advent brings. "When the Church celebrates the liturgy of Advent each year, she makes present this ancient expectancy of the Messiah, for by sharing in the long preparation for the Savior's first coming, the faithful renew their ardent desire for His second coming. By celebrating the precursor's birth and martyrdom, the Church unites herself to His desire: 'He must increase, but I must decrease.'"[27] In this way, these early weeks of Advent highlight John the Baptist as our guide, as one who suffered for a Gospel he probably only scarcely grasped, for a Savior he only sensed. John is the consummate man of good will, the last of the old prophets and the first to leap at the Lord's advent in the womb of Mary.

Mt 3:1–2 (Year A)
Mk 1:1–8 (Year B)
Lk 3:1–6 (Year C)

Where the first week of Advent focused the faithful on the virtue of hope, the traditional theme of the second week of Advent is patience. Patience comes from the Latin verb meaning "to suffer or endure" (*pati*). Is there any more faithful follower of Christ who waited patiently for the advent of God's kingdom than John the Baptist?

Has John the Baptist ever meant really anything to you?

[27] CCC §524.

What emotions or thoughts surface when you think of John or read his words in Scripture?

Ponder the words of the Old Testament this week. Can you relate to the Jewish people's cry for a greater sense of God's presence and power?

Before moving on to John and his message of repentance, let us begin this week by looking at the one who introduces John to Jesus. The second week of Advent will very likely move you from John the Baptist to Mother Mary very quickly, as December 8, the Solemnity of the Immaculate Conception, will probably fall during this week. As Advent brings us back to the beginning of yet another liturgical year, the Immaculate Conception brings us back to the beginnings of Christian salvation, the creation of the New Eve, who alone will grant the Son of God His spotless human nature, with which He shall bind all humanity to Himself.

Whether the Immaculate Conception is celebrated during the last part of the first or the early part of the second week of Advent, there is nothing more fitting during this time of year than to recall the miracle of unborn life, the fidelity of mothers, and the joy that is human birth.

However, there is nothing inherently significant about December 8, and this day's selection for the solemnity really has nothing to do with Advent itself. The Christian calendar normally celebrates the day a saint dies as his or her "birthday" into heaven. That is, the Church usually and prudently waits for a person to have lived the entirety of his or her life on earth before officially declaring that person a saint. But there are three natural birthdays to be celebrated for those who are clearly holy from their beginning, living their *entire* lives in union with God—John the Baptist on June 24 (six months before Christ's birth, cf. Lk 1:26, and fittingly as John "decreases" similarly to the days following the summer solstice, cf. Jn 3:30), of course Jesus on December 25 (who is not a saint but the cause of sanctity itself), and Mary on September 8. When the decision was made to proclaim the absolutely crucial conception of Mary, then, the Church backed up nine months to mark her birthday, making December 8 the day of this celebration.

While there are no canonical Scriptures mentioning Mary's birth, it is found in other very early extra-biblical texts, giving us the names of Anne and Joachim as her parents and describing Our Lady's early life. The liturgical celebration of Mary's conception and birth most likely originated in Jerusalem as early as the fifth century, with more and more attention being paid to Mary after the Council of Ephesus legitimized her title "Mother of God" in 431. Since September 1 marked a new beginning to the calendar year in the East, some historians have argued that September 8 was chosen as Mary's birthday as a sign of how God likewise begins anew. Her immaculate presence marks the inauguration of an entirely new order, and by 1007, the celebration of Mary's birthday had become a universal feast in both the East and the West.

After much medieval reflection and, at times, severe debate, Pope Pius IX (d. 1878) issued his Apostolic Constitution on December 8, 1854, thereby declaring Mary's conception to be free from any taint of original sin through the grace of God. In this way, God preserved a new Eve from whom His Son would join all of humanity back to Himself, thus giving the human race a new opportunity to be rescued from sin and death and thus be joined back to God Himself. Pope Pius wrote:

> We declare, pronounce, and define that the doctrine which holds that the most Blessed Virgin Mary, in the first instance of her conception, by a singular grace and privilege granted by Almighty God, in view of the merits of Jesus Christ, the Savior of the human race, was preserved free from all stain of

> original sin, is a doctrine revealed by God and therefore to be believed firmly and constantly by all the faithful. . . .
>
> Let all the children of the Catholic Church, who are so very dear to us, hear these words of ours. With a still more ardent zeal for piety, religion and love, let them continue to venerate, invoke and pray to the most Blessed Virgin Mary, Mother of God, conceived without original sin. Let them fly with utter confidence to this most sweet Mother of mercy and grace in all dangers, difficulties, needs, doubts and fears. Under her guidance, under her patronage, under her kindness and protection, nothing is to be feared; nothing is hopeless. Because, while bearing toward us a truly motherly affection and having in her care the work of our salvation, she is solicitous about the whole human race. And since she has been appointed by God to be the Queen of heaven and earth, and is exalted above all the choirs of angels and saints, and even stands at the right hand of her only-begotten Son, Jesus Christ our Lord, she presents our petitions in a most efficacious manner. What she asks, she obtains. Her pleas can never be unheard.[28]

As a member of the human race, even Mary the Queen is saved by God's grace (just from the moment of her conception). He is, of course, her savior, and she rightly acknowledges Him as such: "And Mary said: 'My soul proclaims the greatness of the Lord; my spirit rejoices in God my savior'" (Lk 1:46–47). The theology here is the fittingness that if the Son of God was going to unite Himself to each and every human, He needed to receive that humanity from an unsullied and thus universal source. At the start, this is what the first Eve was for the human race on the natural level, and this is what Mary, the New Eve, is on the supernatural today. "When Jesus saw his mother and the disciple there whom he loved, he said to his mother, 'Woman, behold, your son.' Then he said to the disciple, 'Behold, your mother.' And from that hour the disciple took her into his home" (Jn 19:26–27).

---

28 *Ineffabilis Deus* ("The Ineffable God"), thus concluding at this point: "Given at St. Peter's in Rome, the eighth day of December, 1854, in the eighth year of our pontificate. Pius IX."

Predestined from eternity by that decree of divine providence which determined the incarnation of the Word to be the Mother of God, the Blessed Virgin was on this earth the virgin Mother of the Redeemer, and above all others and in a singular way the generous associate and humble handmaid of the Lord. She conceived, brought forth and nourished Christ. She presented Him to the Father in the temple, and was united with Him by compassion as He died on the Cross. In this singular way she cooperated by her obedience, faith, hope and burning charity in the work of the Saviour in giving back supernatural life to souls. Wherefore she is our mother in the order of grace.[29]

When Jesus tells "the disciple" (and not naming "John"), He is telling all disciples to take Mary into their home. Can you hear this call for yourself? How do you take Mary into your home, into your heart?

How do you picture Mary's being conceived immaculately—does God's asking for a sinless mother for His Son make sense to you? How might you explain this dogma to a non-Catholic?

What could you do to increase your affection and time with Mary this Advent?

29 Vatican II's *Lumen Gentium* §61.

One of the later Church Fathers saw how Mary's own immaculateness can even become ours. St. Andrew of Crete (d. 740) was a prolific preacher and focused often on how the true Christian strives to grow closer to Christ through the maternal love of Mary. In this particular sermon, he has us imagine how God restores the beauty of the human race, that one visible creature made in His own image and likeness, by beginning with Mary's immaculate humanity. As such, God not only restores humanity to what Adam and Eve were before the Fall (even if concupiscence remains) but in fact elevates us to a divinized state, a godliness in which we can all partake.

Take some time during your prayer period to ponder this ancient homily slowly, stopping wherever you feel the inspiration to take in a word or image more deeply.

> Today, humanity recovers the gift it had received when first formed by divine hands, and returns immaculate to its original nobility. The shame of sin had cast a shadow upon the splendor and charm of human nature; but when the Mother of Him Who is Beauty itself is born, this nature recovers in her person its ancient privileges, and is fashioned according to a perfect model, truly worthy of God. And this fashioning is a perfect restoration; this restoration is a divinization, and this divinization is an assimilation to the primitive state. . . . In a word, the reformation of our nature begins today; the world, which had grown old, undergoes a transformation which is wholly divine, and receives the first fruits of its second creation.
>
> Who indeed was this Virgin and from what sort of parents did she come? Mary, the glory of all, was born of the tribe of David, and from the seed of Joachim. She was descended from Eve, and was the child of Anna. Joachim was a gentle man, pious, raised in God's law. Living prudently and walking before God he grew old without child: the years of his prime provided no continuation of his lineage. Anna was likewise God-loving, prudent, but barren; she lived in harmony with her husband, but was childless. As much concerned about

this, as about the observance of the law of the Lord, she indeed was daily stung by the grief of childlessness and suffered that which is the usual lot of the childless—she grieved, she sorrowed, she was distressed, and impatient at being childless.

Thus, Joachim and his spouse lamented that they had no successor to continue their line; yet the spark of hope was not extinguished in them completely: both intensified their prayer about the granting to them of a child to continue their line. In imitation of the prayer heard of Hannah (cf. 1 Kgs 1:10), both without leaving the temple fervently beseeched God that He would undo her sterility and make fruitful her childlessness. And they did not give up on their efforts, until their wish be fulfilled. The Bestower of Gifts did not condemn the gift of their hope. The unceasing power came quickly in help to those praying and beseeching God, and it made capable both the one and the other to produce and bear a child. In such manner, from sterile and barren parents, as it were from irrigated trees, was borne for us a most glorious fruition—the Immaculate Virgin.

Thus the immaculate fruition issuing forth from the womb occurred from an infertile mother, and then the parents, in the first blossoming of her growth brought her to the temple and dedicated her to God. The priest, then offering the order of services, beheld the face of the girl, and he became gladdened and joyful, seeing as it were the actual fulfillment of the Divine promise.[30]

What struck you here, and why do you think the Holy Spirit had you linger there?

God wants to save you by making you like Himself. Does this

[30] St. Andrew of Crete (d. 740), *Homily 1 on Mary's Nativity*; *The Dogma of the Immaculate Conception*, ed. Edward O'Connor (South Bend: University of Notre Dame Press, 2017), 118–19.

reality of becoming "divinized" mean anything to you? Where would you most like to become like Jesus?

Is the power of Mary's faith and her trust in the Father becoming more and more real for you?

How has Mary played a role in your spirituality so far? How might you offer her a more active role at this point in your life? What would that mean for you?

> O mortal, you now know that God has become flesh. But how did this Incarnation come to be? This occurrence is owed to the Holy Virgin's body. She is one with us and we should therefore cry out with joy. We should celebrate the world's mysterious salvation, which is the new birth of all of us. For today the curse of Adam ends. It is no longer, "For you are dust, and to dust you shall return" (Gen 3:19), but you have now been united with heaven and into heaven you will be exalted. To Eve it is no longer, "In pain you shall bring forth children" (Gen 3:16), but now, blessed is she who brought Emmanuel forth, and "Blessed is the womb that carried him" (Lk 11:27).[31]

Whereas in the old order the First Adam gives way to the First Eve, now the Second Eve gives flesh to the New Adam, the One

---

[31] St. Basil the Great (d. 379), *Homily on the Generation of Christ;* editor's translation.

who has come from heaven to be joined to our impoverished state through the humble "yes" of a lowly virgin.

Lest you think that all this talk of a New Adam and a New Eve is possibly muddying your prayer with highfalutin dogma, know that this is ancient language and, in one sense, the basis of the Christian faith. Mature spirituality and holy theology go hand-in-hand—spirituality without good doctrine is mere emotion, and theology without spirituality is just academic inanity. The original innocence of Mary is at the heart of Jesus's mission to unite Himself to every man and woman, because it is from her immaculate humanity that He is receives the rest of us. Just as we were all somehow "contained" in the first mother of all, and with her and from her we all turned away from God, in Mary we are all regathered as spiritual children and thus made, as the Ancients used to say, *filii in Filio*—sons and daughters in her Son.

One of the most commonly written icons in Christianity is the *Deisis*, from a Greek word meaning "a prayer of supplication." In the center of this icon is the radiantly resurrected Christ, flanked by the Virgin Mother on one side and John the Baptist on the other. In some sense, these two, along with Elizabeth, were the first to greet the Son of God into this world. John was thus consecrated from the womb, forging the trajectory of the rest of his life—one not at all content with the world, who went off to the desert to live a life of prayer and austerity, who eventually found himself jailed and eventually martyred defending the sanctity of husband and wife. John hence found his true self and calling from the nuptial union between God and Mary; he gave himself in defense of the integrity of marriage as God Himself intended.

Saint Augustine was originally trained as a professional rhetor, one who would use the powerful sway of oratory to achieve financially lucrative results in the court of law as well as in the court of public opinion. Although he finally left that world and lived undividedly for Christ, his love of words and understanding of the power of rhetoric never left him, but was consecrated for the kingdom. In preaching on Jesus as the Word of God and John the Baptist as the voice crying out in the desert, Augustine plays with the interchange between word and voice:

> John a voice, the Lord, however, *in the beginning was the Word* (Jn 1:1). John a voice for a time, Christ the eternal Word in the beginning. Take away the word, and what is a voice? Where there is no meaning, it's just an empty noise. A voice without a word knocks at the ear, it doesn't build up the intellect. All the same, in the business of building up our intellects, let's observe the order of things. If I'm thinking what I am to say, there is already a word in my mind; but as I wish to speak to you, I look for a way of how what is already in my mind may also be found in yours. Looking for this way of how the word that is already in my mind may reach you and lodge in your mind, I take hold of my voice, and with the voice I've taken hold of I speak to you. The sound of my voice conducts to you the understanding of my word; and when the sound of the voice has conducted to you the understanding of the word, the sound is indeed over and done with; but the word which the sound conducted to you is now in your mind, and hasn't departed from mine.[32]

Do you appreciate the Church Fathers' insistence that the fullness of Catholic worship demands the "building up of our intellect"? What doctrines or practices is God asking you to study or develop further after this retreat?

Augustine here argues that words must be made external by the voice. Do you give voice to your most inner thoughts, or do you tend not to speak up or reveal what is going on inside? When and why do you not open up more, and when and why might you say too much? Is your speech everywhere and

32 St. Augustine, *Sermon* 293.3 (preached 413); trans. Edmund Hill, *Sermons (273–305A)* (Hyde Park: New City Press, 1994), 150.

always guided by truth and the refusal neither to break nor bend the truth?

Augustine continues:

> Do you want to see the voice disappearing, and the divinity of the Word remaining? John's baptism—where is it now? It performed its service and departed. Now it's Christ's baptism that is frequented. We all believe in Christ, we all hope for salvation in Christ; that's the Word the sound of the voice conveyed. It's difficult, you see, to distinguish word from voice, and that's why John himself was thought to be the Christ. The voice was thought to be the Word; but the voice identified himself, in order not to offend the Word. *I am not,* he said, *the Christ, nor Elijah, nor the prophet.*[33]

Does Augustine's thought make sense to you? The word precedes the voice, and once spoken, the voice diminishes, but the word remains. Whereas John first preached repentance, Christ came to bring royal sonship. Do you mark your Christian life and growth in holiness by the sins you avoid or by how much you are becoming more and more like Christ?

How often our words reveal our inner selves. Our speech can be flippant and insincere, or our words can be full of integrity and purpose. "Therefore, putting away falsehood, speak the truth, each one to his neighbor, for we are members one of another" (Eph 4:25). Everyone in our lives deserves the truth when spoken to, and those

33 Ibid.

closest to us deserve some level of insight into our inner lives. Words allow us to imitate the Word of God by making known externally (the Incarnation) what has been going on internally (the Trinity). That is, Jesus comes to us at this time of the year to reveal what He has always known—the love of the Father.

The word *obedience* means "to listen to another's words," and it is one of the religious vows that consecrated men and women have professed for centuries. While you may not belong to a religious community, all the baptized are called to listen to God. In fact, when you were baptized, the priest or deacon touched your ears and your mouth, praying over you in one of the words of Christ still left in his original Aramaic in the Bible, *ephphatha*, commanding "be opened" (Mk 7:34). So, in one sense, your Christian life began with this command: "*Ephphatha*: that is, be opened, that you may profess the faith you hear, to the praise and glory of God."

When St. Benedict began the first monastery in the West, he composed his *Rule* in order to keep all those living there mindful of the life they had each freely undertaken. His insistence on listening is a very needed reminder for us today, who seem always to have something or someone in our ears:

> Then let us arise! Scripture invites us in the words, "It is full time now for you to wake from sleep" (Rom 13:11). With our eyes open to the light that transfigures, our ears filled with the thunder of his voice, let us listen to the powerful voice of God, urging us day by day, "Oh, that today you would hearken to his voice! Harden not your hearts" (Ps 95:8). And again: "He who has an ear, let him hear what the Spirit says to the churches" (Rev 2:7). And what does he say? "Come, O children, listen to me, I will teach you the fear of the Lord" (Ps 34:11). "Walk while you have the light, lest the darkness overtake you" (Jn 12:35). Moreover the Lord, in seeking among the crowd for someone to work for him, says, "Who is there who desires life?" (Ps 34:12). If you hear him and answer, "I do," God says to you, "Do you desire true life, eternal life?" then: "Keep your tongue from evil, and your lips from speaking deceit. Depart from evil, and do good; seek peace, and pursue it" (Ps 34:13–14). And

> when you have done this, I will set my eyes upon you, I will give ear to your prayers, and "Before they call, I will answer" (Is 65:24).[34]

It's an intriguing trajectory Benedict sketches at the beginning of his *Rule*: what one hears influences how one speaks, which, in turn, fashions one's desires. "Do you desire true life?" Benedict asks. If so, this desire will be born not out of deceit and sloppy practices of listening to whatever one wants; no, this desire will be fostered by keeping our "lips from speaking deceit," which also demands that we give our "ears to prayer."

Do you "waste" your listening on words or music that do not unite you ever closer to God and the things of God? Do you have to have noise consistently in your ears, even unconsciously?

Have you noticed how your desires can easily be shaped by the cultural and social influences and fads of the day? What strategies have you learned to keep "the world" from forming what it is you truly want?

Let us now once more pray over another homily from St. Augustine, where he again juxtaposes John with Jesus, here moving our attention from the birth of these two to their respective deaths:

> So we've heard that Christ is the Word; let us hear that John is the voice. When he was asked, *You then, who are you? he answered, I am the voice of one crying in the desert* (Jn 1:22–23).

---

34 Benedict of Nursia (d. 550), *The Monastic Rule, Prologue* (composed c. 530); Clément, *The Roots of Christian Mysticism*, 24.

> So if Christ is the Word, John the voice, John was taken over as the voice in order that the Word might be spoken to us; and that the Word might come to us, the voice preceded it. That's why it's both true that Christ was before John in eternity, and that all the same, he had not to be born first, unless John came to us before the Word as the voice. So there is going to be a time when we shall see the Word as he is seen by the angels; now, however, let us make progress in the Word, so that we may remain with him for ever.
>
> But *he must grow, I must diminish; but he must grow, I must diminish* (Jn 3:30). This was apparent even from the very births of the Word and of the voice. The Word was born on 25 December, from which point the day begins to increase; the voice was born before the Word of God, when the day begins to diminish. *He must grow,* he said, *I, however, must diminish.* And their deaths also showed this. John was diminished by having his head cut off; Christ grew, by being raised up on the cross. And so, brothers and sisters, let us celebrate the birthday of the voice in honor of the Word; not in drunkenness and revelry (Rom 13:13), as the apostle says, but everything whatsoever you do, do it in the name of God (Col 3:17), and the God of peace will be with you (Phil 4:9).[35]

Did Augustine preach this with a bit of a smirk? Did his congregation conceal their chuckles, or could one hear a laugh or two? Jesus increases upon death because He is lifted high on a cross, whereas John diminishes because he has his head lopped off. Clever and witty as this may be, the paradox is apparent: When we practice mortifications of any sort, Jesus's fullness is able to increase the grace in our souls—we "diminish" through prayer and fasting and acts of charity in order that He has more and more room to fill up in our souls.

---

[35] St. Augustine, *Sermon* 293A.5 (date preached uncertain; placed here in Augustine's works only because of its continued theme of John the Baptist); trans. Edmund Hill, Sermons (273–305A), 161–62. Note that the translation of "25 December" here is actually "on the 8 of the Kalends of January" in the original Latin.

This is why the second week of Advent is dedicated to patience, that willingness to stand under any trial with Christlike joy and the meekness that alone can receive such joy. Let us once again turn, then, to Benedict's *Rule*, focusing on the need for humility and how that can grow throughout our lifetime.

> If we wish to attain the summit of humility, we must by our actions set up the ladder that appeared in a dream to Jacob and on which he saw angels descending and ascending. This descent and ascent show us that by trying to climb we descend and by humility we ascend. Now, this ladder thus set up is our life in this world, and when the heart is humbled the Lord raises it to heaven. The sides of the ladder are our body and soul, and on these sides God's call has fixed the steps of humility for us to climb. . . . The first degree of humility consists in always keeping present in the mind the fear of God and absolutely avoiding forgetfulness of it. . . .
>
> The second degree of humility is not to love one's own will, not to take pleasure in fulfilling one's own desires, but in one's actions to imitate the Lord when he says: "I have come down from heaven, not to do my own will, but the will of him who sent me" (Jn 6:38). . . .
>
> The third degree of humility is to subject oneself in all obedience to a superior for the love of God, imitating the Lord of whom the apostle says: "He became obedient unto death" (Phil 2:8).
>
> The fourth degree of humility consists in keeping patience and tranquility of spirit, even when hard and repugnant commands are given or one is unjustly treated.[36]

The Latin word for mortal man (*homo*) and the word for humility (*humilitas*) come from the same root word meaning earth or soil (*humus*), telling us a lot about what this virtue entails—to be honest with oneself and to admit that one is only human, not

[36] St. Benedict of Nursia (d. 550), *The Monastic Rule* §7; Clément, *The Roots of Christian Mysticism*, 156.

a god or goddess, and that from earth we have come and into earth each of our bodies will inevitably descend.

How do you define humility, and what does it mean for your everyday living and understanding of yourself and those around you?

Looking at Benedict's first four rules of growing in humility, speak to the Holy Spirit about his four points here:

1. How do I keep God in mind throughout my day? How might I be able to grow in prayerfulness?
2. When making a decision, what do I prioritize—the outcome regardless of the action, or praying over how Jesus would respond in such a situation, regardless of the outcome?
3. To whom do I subject your will? This may not be a constant, but who in my life do I trust to follow, and why?
4. Is my deepest spirit mostly at rest? Am I able to detect patterns of tranquility and unquiet? Try to jot these moments down and pray over when they started, why they started, and what you might do to decrease the anxieties and increase the consolations.

Hilary of Poitiers was a fourth-century bishop in modern-day France who—like many of us—did not take Christ too seriously in the beginning of his adult life but instead ran after money, comfort, and convenience. He quickly discovered, however, that this left him empty and restless. He wanted to do something more with his energies and give himself over to a life that would not depend on the ups and downs of this world but would instead continue over into life eternal. When he was looking back on this early search for the meaning of life, he recalled how he was at first strongly drawn to a life and career which would result in an abundance of material comforts:

> Although these things contain, indeed, the highest and most pleasant luxuries of life, they do not seem to differ much from the pleasures of animals, that are free from work and are sated with food, as they roam about in the forests or in the rich pastures. . . . Many people, it seems to me, have rejected this degrading and bestial manner of living in their own case and despised it in that of others for no other reason than that under the inspiration of nature itself they believed it unbecoming for man to be born only for the sake of his belly and idleness, and that they have not entered this life from any desire of devoting themselves to noble deeds or to a good occupation, or that this very life has been granted to them without any gain for eternity.[37]

Do you ever have those deep, late-night discussions on the meaning of life? Here is a helpful way to think about such an important question: If our life were made just to take in nutrients, as the gluttonous gourmand might argue, we would be no different than plants. If our life were all about pleasing our senses and filling our bodies with the best, and relaxing in the most comfortable, we would be no different than brute animals. But Hilary sensed there is a higher life, a life that is not simply "natural" but must be supernatural—a life of noble deeds and eternal reward.

---

37 St. Hilary of Poitiers (d. 367), *The Trinity*, opening lines of Book 1; trans. Stephen McKenna, *Saint Hilary of Poitiers: The Trinity* (Washington, DC: Catholic University of America Press, [1954] 2002), 4–5.

How do you understand the essence of your life here on earth? Do you live it nobly and with eternity in mind?

Did you ever go through a period of wondering what life was about? Where was God in that time, and what did you learn?

Have you ever noticed how quickly a building can be razed, but how long an architectural beauty takes to go up? Have you yet noticed how painstaking it is for you to grow in a virtue, but how quickly you can snap and lose your temper, overindulge in food and drink, or simply give up? In our fallen world, decay and destruction and death are the natural tendencies of things and are therefore realized in no time. Splendor, virtue, and true life, however, take time, and not being natural but supernatural, they also require grace. We have been made for a joy that surpasses our natural human capabilities.

This is why the Church Fathers wrote so much on patience and our need to wait on the Lord, a theme the Scriptures present over and over:

> Be still before the Lord; wait for him. Do not be provoked by the prosperous, nor by malicious schemers. (Ps 37:7)

> Rejoice in hope, endure in affliction, persevere in prayer. (Rom 12:12)

> Have no anxiety at all, but in everything, by prayer and petition, with thanksgiving, make your requests known to God. (Eph 4:6)

When one thinks of a saint or even a great-souled man or woman, one has a hard time imagining that person as hotheaded or inordinately raging when impatient. The early martyrs knew better than any the power of the divine gift of patience. As unjustly accused and maltreated as they were, those going to their death for Christ knew that while it might be easy to lash out and try to save one's skin, a greater reward awaited them if they could only imitate the Crucified God:

> It is the wholesome precept of our Lord and Master: He that endures, says He, *unto the end, the same shall be saved* (Mt 10:22) and again, *If you continue, says He, in my word, you shall be truly my disciples; and you shall know the truth, and the truth shall make you free* (Jn 8:31–32). We must endure and persevere, beloved brethren, in order that, being admitted to the hope of truth and liberty, we may attain to the truth and liberty itself; for that very fact that we are Christians is the substance of faith and hope. But that hope and faith may attain to their result, there is need of patience. For we are not following after present glory, but future. . . .
>
> Charity is the bond of brotherhood, the foundation of peace, the holdfast and security of unity, which is greater than both hope and faith, which excels both good works and martyrdoms, which will abide with us always, eternal with God in the kingdom of heaven. Take from it patience; and deprived of it, it does not endure. Take from it the substance of bearing and of enduring, and it continues with no roots nor strength. The apostle, finally, when he would speak of charity, joined to it endurance and patience. Charity, he says, is large-souled; *charity is kind; charity envies not, is not puffed up, is not provoked, thinks not evil; loves all things, believes all things, hopes all things, bears all things* (1 Cor 13:4–7). Thence he shows that it can tenaciously persevere, because it knows how to endure all things. And in another place: *Forbearing one another,* he says, *in love, using every effort to keep the unity of the spirit in the bond of peace* (Eph 4:2–3). He proved that neither unity nor peace could be kept unless brethren should cherish one another with

mutual toleration, and should keep the bond of concord by the intervention of patience.[38]

As this week holds our attention on John the Baptist, we are to keep the theology of patience and humility in mind. For here is a man who spent his life waiting for another and proclaiming a kingdom he himself would not experience while alive; here is a man who laid his own life down in defense of marriage as God intends and not someone who ever made it about his own success or comfort. But the greatest thing about John was how he spent his life waiting in exile for a God he knew would come, and this is the Good News of this week's readings and prayer: God is nearing and promises to be present in all we are and are about.

That is why these first two weeks of Advent recall over and over the long history of Israel, God's first covenanted people. In that salvation history, John serves as the bridge between the Old and the New, realizing the One whom all the prophets awaited. By the grace of God—from the womb—John realized that God's chosen people would not be saved by a political potentate but by a sacrificial lamb who could be received only by the penitent: "I am the voice of one crying out in the desert, make straight the way of the Lord" (Is 40:3 as at Jn 1:23). John's whole life had been spent here in anticipation of the sacrifice that would save mankind: "Behold, the Lamb of God, who takes away the sin of the world" (Is 53:7 as at Jn 1:29).

The "Father of Church History" and a fourth-century bishop of the important diocese of Caesarea, Eusebius, was a careful thinker and an early example of a Christian able to discern God's activity in the most mundane of human events. When commenting on the book of Isaiah, he could not help but understand the prophet's message fully without seeing its completion in the life of John the Baptist. This is how all the early Christians read Scripture: the Old would be fulfilled and completely understood only in

---

38 St. Cyprian of Carthage (d. 258), *On the Value of Patience* [Treatise IX], §13 and 15, New Advent translation: https://www.newadvent.org/fathers/050709.htm.

the New Testament, and the truths there would be fully realized only in heaven. Eusebius thus writes:

> The voice of one crying in the wilderness: Prepare the way of the Lord, make straight the paths of our God. The prophecy makes clear that it is to be fulfilled, not in Jerusalem but in the wilderness: it is there that the glory of the Lord is to appear, and God's salvation is to be made known to all mankind. It was in the wilderness that God's saving presence was proclaimed by John the Baptist, and there that God's salvation was seen. The words of this prophecy were fulfilled when Christ and his glory were made manifest to all: after his baptism the heavens opened, and the Holy Spirit in the form of a dove rested on him, and the Father's voice was heard, bearing witness to the Son: This is my beloved Son, listen to him. The prophecy meant that God was to come to a deserted place, inaccessible from the beginning. None of the pagans had any knowledge of God, since his holy servants and prophets were kept from approaching them. The voice commands that a way be prepared for the Word of God: the rough and trackless ground is to be made level, so that our God may find a highway when he comes. Prepare the way of the Lord: the way is the preaching of the Gospel, the new message of consolation, ready to bring to all mankind the knowledge of God's saving power.[39]

Perhaps the desert scenery John the Baptist inevitably brings does not speak to you very much. That is fine, as most of us will never know what it is like to dwell in a real desert or even in a very desolate place. Yet we all have those places of dryness and darkness in our lives. We all carry triggers and traumas that lurk under our facades of self-possession; we all have sins that are still hidden, which we fear to call out. But perhaps preparing a path for the Lord and making straight His way means to acknowledge those places which are still far from God—wrestling with some past pain or

---

39 Eusebius of Caesarea (d. 339), *Commentary on Isaiah*, ch. 40, found in the *Liturgy of the Hours*, vol. I, Advent Season & Christmas Season (New York: Catholic Book Publishing Co., 1975), 202.

naming our worst sin(s) in the sacrament of Reconciliation. Perhaps it means to bring down the proud places of our soul, which we are afraid to touch because we have spent so much time and energy building ourselves up there; perhaps it means lifting up the valleys of pain and fear where we have sunk or been pushed down. This is the week, then, to make our hearts smooth and level, fit to receive the Lord when He at last comes.

What is the "wilderness" in your life—that is, where might you feel out of control, alone, or abandoned? Why might God allow you to be there?

Do you allow yourself to remain in that deserted place or do you fill in any moment of stillness with diversions, time on your phone, and actively ignore the deeper questions of life?

What does it mean for you to make a path straight? What in your life needs correction, or who is in your life that the Lord might be asking you to help right now?

When did you last make a good confession? Perhaps, at this point in the second week of Advent, you might consider reviewing your life and taking notes on those major moments of moral failure and bringing that list to the sacrament of Reconciliation, where you can hear Jesus Himself (through His ordained priest) say directly to you, "And I absolve you of your sins, in the Name of the Father, and of the Son, and of the Holy Spirit."

The word John the Baptist used for his command to all of us to repent was *metanoia*, a compound term literally meaning to change (*meta*) one's way of thinking (*nous*). Authentic conversion thus begins with the mind, not necessarily the morals; in other words, before one is convinced of God's love and mercy, no determination or regiment to change one's ways will really last too long. Every human person is an eternal composite of body and soul, and while we might change some bodily actions for a time, until our mind is purposefully dedicated and desirous of an unchanging good, no real change takes place:

> Jesus summoned the crowd and said to them, "Hear and understand. It is not what enters one's mouth that defiles that person; but what comes out of the mouth is what defiles one." (Mt 15:11)

> He said to them, "Are even you likewise without understanding? Do you not realize that everything that goes into a person from outside cannot defile, since it enters not the heart but the stomach and passes out into the latrine?" (Thus he declared all foods clean.) "But what comes out of a person, that is what defiles. From within people, from their hearts, come evil thoughts, unchastity, theft, murder, adultery, greed, malice, deceit, licentiousness, envy, blasphemy, arrogance, folly. All these evils come from within and they defile." (Mk 7:18–23)

To receive the Christ Child at Christmas, the Church thus begins the season with our need to repent. Repent of what? "I am a good person—I don't steal, I don't kill," and so on. But comparing ourselves to those in the news or those moral monsters of the Third Reich will always result in complacency and a distorted opinion of our own goodness. Let us instead compare ourselves to the saints—to John the Baptist or even Mary. Then we shall begin to realize our need to grow more and more open to the grace of holiness.

Extended Prayer Period. Do you make monthly confession a regular practice? To grow in holiness is also to grow in awareness of our own brokenness. The more we allow the light to shine upon us, the more the shadows appear, and in Christ, that is not a defeat but a victory. It is how we are convinced of sin by the Holy Spirit, who points things out to us so we can then place them in Christ's pierced hands through the sacrament of Reconciliation. A good examination of conscience can assist us in this movement from becoming aware of our sins, naming them, and then bringing them to Jesus in the confessional.

First Commandment: I am the Lord your God; you shall not have strange Gods before me.

An idol is a false image of God, one that we have put upon the true reality. What idols do you still hold on to? How do you understand God? Is He one who punishes you when you err and rewards you when you try to be good? That is an idol that has to be smashed. Do you imagine God as one who is always disappointed in you, always demanding more? That is an idol that has to be smashed. Can you simply rest with Jesus in knowing the Father's unmerited and undeserved love?

When looking at how you spend your day, what consumes your energies more than God? Have you made a savior out of your finances, your social status, your bodily comforts? How could you more practically give God His due place as absolute Lord and Sovereign, and not just an afterthought or one to whom you go only when you are in need of something?

Second Commandment: You shall not take the name of the Lord your God in vain.

Do you tend to use the Lord's name when upset or shocked? How could you better follow Jesus's own command to keep "hallowed" the Father's name and His?

Do you watch your speech to make sure it is edifying and always truthful? Are you aware of the sin of scandal and giving a bad example by the words you choose?

Third Commandment: Remember to keep holy the Lord's Day.

Do you faithfully get to Mass each and every Sunday or Saturday Vigil? Do you make sure to keep the holy days of obligation by getting to Mass (January 1, the Ascension, August 15, November 1, December 8, and December 25) and following the fasts and abstinences of Lent?

How do you make each day "holy"? Are you faithful to daily prayer and some sort of examination of conscience? Do you seek closer union with Christ through daily devotions, spiritual reading, as well as fasting and almsgiving in whatever way is appropriate to both the season of the Church as well as your own state in life?

Fourth Commandment: Honor your father and your mother.

Have I striven to be grateful to my father and mother for my existence? Have I sought to honor them through being available to help them when and where appropriate, praying for them, and thanking them for who I have become? Have I truly forgiven my father and mother when they were not perfect?

Do I look down on those older than I for being slower and no longer as capable, getting frustrated with how it affects me and my time? Have I ever felt the Holy Spirit's nudging me to be more attentive to the aged, perhaps even visiting or bringing Holy Communion to shut-ins and those in nursing homes?

Fifth Commandment: You shall not kill.

Have I ever directly or indirectly aided in the taking of human life? Do I ever find myself rejoicing in the death of another, whether someone I knew personally or a perceived enemy on the news?

Have I ever freely harmed another, even through words or my thoughts? Have I ever found myself rejoicing in another's misfortunes? Have I ever objectified another person based on his or her nationality, skin color, or any other reason?

Sixth Commandment: You shall not commit adultery.

Am I always faithful to my spouse, physically as well as emotionally? Have I objectified another sexually, reducing that person to a "thing" only for my pleasure? Do I entertain impure images on my phone or computer? Do I guard my senses and turn away or turn off any crude music, shows, or even ads? Do I live and dress chastely, giving good example to those around me?

Have I ever given in to masturbation or any other kind of unfruitfully selfish arousal? Have I ever used artificial contraception, in-vitro fertilization, or any other act condemned by Christ and His Church?

Seventh Commandment: You shall not steal.

Have I ever taken anything that I knew did not belong to me? Do I justify the taking of small things by fooling myself that it won't be missed or that it was just going to be discarded anyway? Does my pay reflect my hours of work, or do I inflate my recorded activity? Have I ever failed to live up to a contract?

Am I ever kind or good to someone out of financial motivation? Do I seek to live in a simple and evangelical manner appropriate to my state in life? Do I find myself constantly worrying about finances and my comfort level?

Eighth Commandment: You shall not bear false witness against your neighbor.

Have I ever lied about someone? Have I ever told the truth about someone only to distract from that person's right to a good reputation? Do I ever rejoice in the bad news surrounding another's misfortune?

Am I ever guilty of rash judgment, especially against someone whose lifestyle I condemn? Do I ever partake in hurtful gossip and fail to stand up for another when being uncharitably talked about?

Ninth Commandment: You shall not covet your neighbor's spouse.

Do I ever look lustfully at others with whom I spend my day—a neighbor or coworker? If married, do I honor my spouse with heartfelt affection and am faithful to him or her—physically as well as emotionally—especially in rough times?

Do I ever flirt or use sexual humor to change the conversation to the erotic? Have I ever talked to others about the sensuality of another? Have I ever been overly curious about the sex or emotional life of another?

Tenth Commandment: You shall not covet your neighbor's goods.

Do I find myself constantly envious of another's riches? Am I content with my own state in life, or do I always compare my possessions with others? Have I ever defaced or marred another's possession out of malice?

Do I squander money through loose spending or gambling? Do I watch my consumption level and try to live in accord with Gospel simplicity? Do I tithe or make room in my budget for the less fortunate? Am I grateful for all that I have?

Supplemental Reading: TAN Books, *Confession: Its Fruitful Practice with an Examination of Conscience*

Week 3

The Joy of Advent

To be prayed from the first Sunday of Advent until Christmas Eve

℣. The Angel of the Lord brought tidings unto Mary
℟. And she conceived by the Holy Spirit.

Let us pray.

Pour forth we beseech Thee, O Lord, Thy grace into our hearts, that we to whom the Incarnation of Christ, Thy Son, was made known by the message of an Angel, may, by his Passion and Cross, be brought to the glory of his Resurrection. Through the same Christ, our Lord.
℟. Amen.

You will most likely be struck by the rose vestments on the Third Sunday of Advent. This is *Gaudete*, or "Rejoice," Sunday. The Christian concept of joy is found in the first triad of the twelve fruits of the Holy Spirit—love, joy, and peace (cf. Gal 5:22–23)—and is nothing other than the gift of Christ living his own life within each of us. "Christ was anointed with the oil of gladness, that is, with the Holy Spirit. The Spirit is so called because he is the source of joy. You also, you have received the sacramental anointing [at your

Sacrament of Confirmation]. You have in this way become companions and partakers of Christ."[40]

The Gospel this week will show John the Baptist as embodying the two aspects of Christian discipleship. You will see how he is either hard at work baptizing and teaching the crowds about the Messiah, or you will meet him in prison, still and patiently being with God in prayer. Those two ways of being a Christian must feed off each other in your own life as well: never be so busy you do not take time for prayer and adoration; never be so still you neglect the duties of charity to those who make up all the blessings of your particular life.

Mt 11:2–11 (Year A)
Jn 1:6–8,19–28 (Year B)
Lk 3:10–18 (Year C)

The readings today will also exhort us to rejoice. "Rejoice in the Lord always. I shall say it again: rejoice!" (Phil 4:4). Our Savior is ever nearer, only two weeks or so to go, and God Himself will be forever visible and present to all of our senses. For now, only Mary can feel Him in her tabernacled womb; only she knows fully how this child has come to be, but she is inviting each of us to prepare to behold the source and the summit of our joy, of our deepest desires finally being realized.

How do you define joy? Is it essentially different from how you understand happiness?

Why does the Christian tradition place joy alongside love and peace? How do you understand this connection, and where in your life do you experience it—the joy of knowing you are your

[40] St. Cyril of Jerusalem, *Mystagogical Catecheses*, III.2; Clément, *The Roots of Christian Mysticism*, 106.

beloved's and he or she is yours, and the peace of knowing this bond of love is eternal?

Where in your life do you want to ask the Father to increase your joy?

Although St. Thomas Aquinas is not a Church Father but a medieval Doctor of the Church, he drew constantly from the best thinkers of the early Church, and in his great work the *Summa Theologiae*, he asks whether joy is caused by love, and his answer is well worth quoting here:

> For joy is caused by love, either through the presence of the thing loved, or because the proper good of the thing loved exists and endures in it; and the latter is the case chiefly in the love of benevolence, whereby a man rejoices in the well-being of his friend, though he be absent. On the other hand, sorrow arises from love, either through the absence of the thing loved, or because the loved object to which we wish well, is deprived of its good or afflicted with some evil. Now charity is love of God, whose good is unchangeable, since he is his goodness, and from the very fact that he is loved, he is in those who love him by his most excellent effect, according to 1 John 4:16: "He that abideth in charity, abideth in God, and God in him." Therefore spiritual joy, which is about God, is caused by charity.[41]

Appreciate the connection traced here: joy comes from love, which is the result of being present to another. This is why God has

41 St. Thomas Aquinas (d. 1274), *Summa Theologiae*, II–II.28.1, New Advent translation: https://www.newadvent.org/summa/3028.htm.

become man and what this season of Advent is to prepare in us: the Lord is drawing near to be present to each of us in a bond of love so we may experience the fullness of joy. "As the Father loves me, so I also love you. Remain in my love. If you keep my commandments, you will remain in my love, just as I have kept my Father's commandments and remain in his love. I have told you this so that my joy may be in you and your joy may be complete" (Jn 15:9–11).

Aquinas here naturally contrasts joy with sorrow. Joy is caused by presence, sorrow by separation. In this way, joy is relational: it neither originates nor ends in oneself. It is caused by the existence of one not myself and terminates in the union the presence of that person gives me. True joy comes not from successes or self-mastery but from the vulnerability and transparency only deep interpersonal union can elicit.

Is this not why Jesus instituted the Eucharist, the unmatchable manner by which He continues to remain with us, soul and divinity, body and blood? This is why every season in the liturgical year must be Eucharistic. The Lord draws near, not just in memory and story, but truly and really in the Most Blessed Sacrament. Here His incarnation continues; here the angels continue to gather above in awe and adoration; here the world can come to understand what it is meant to be.

> It was recognized, in fact, that this glorious flesh possessed the property common to all human beings: like them it was maintained with the help of bread. But this body partook of the divine dignity because of the indwelling of the Word. We are therefore entitled to believe that the bread hallowed by the Word of God is transformed to become the body of the Word. . . . As the bread transformed into that body was thereby raised to divine power, a similar change happens to the bread of the Eucharist. In the former case the grace of the Word hallowed the body that drew its substance from bread, and in a sense was itself bread. Likewise in the Eucharist the bread is hallowed by the Word of God and prayer. . . . It is transformed at once into his body . . . as expressed in these words: "This is my body." . . . That is why, in the economy of grace, he gives

> himself as seed to all the faithful. His flesh composed of bread and wine is blended with their bodies to enable human beings, thanks to their union with his immortal body, to share in the condition of incorruptibility.[42]

"We are fed with the bread from heaven, our thirst is quenched by the cup of joy, the chalice afire with the Spirit, the blood wholly warmed from on high by the Spirit."[43] Remember, the "bread" you approach at Mass is not just bread, but the taste and the feel and the sight of bread is united to a deeper reality—namely, the divinity of Jesus Christ. Just as Jesus "looked" like every other Jewish man of His day, underneath that hair and skin was the Son of God. Holy Communion is nothing different: beneath the appearances of bread and wine is the reality of the Most Holy Body and Blood of the Son of God.

> Let us approach the altar with burning desire and with our hands folded in the form of a cross, let us receive the body of the Crucified; and applying our eyes and lips and foreheads let us partake of the divine coal (cf. Isaiah 6), so that the fire of the desire within us might receive the heat of the coal and burn up our sins and illuminate our hearts, and so that by partaking of the divine fire we might be set on fire and deified. Isaiah saw a coal, and a coal is not plain wood but wood united with fire. In the same way the bread of communion is not plain bread but bread united with divinity. For the body united with divinity is not a single nature, but that of the body is one nature and that of the divinity united with it is another nature. Consequently, both together are not one nature but two.[44]

---

42 Gregory of Nyssa, *Catechetical Oration* 37; Clément, *The Roots of Christian Mysticism*, 109–10.

43 An anonymous homily inspired by Hippolytus of Rome's *Treatise on Easter, Exordium* §8; Clément, *The Roots of Christian Mysticism*, 113.

44 John of Damascus (d. 749), *On the Orthodox Faith* §86; trans. Norman Russell, *On the Orthodox Faith* (Yonkers: St. Vladimir's Seminary Press, 2022), 251, slightly adjusted. Note that in older editions, this is cited as *On the Orthodox Faith* 4.13.

Do you ever pray to be near loved ones at the moment of Holy Communion, to be mystically present to those who have gone before you, to estranged family members and old friends, but especially even closer to those around you at Mass right then and there? Holy Communion is the bond of charity, the one act that unites us with both God and neighbor. To whom do you need to grow closer?

In English, we often confuse two words that should really be understood separately—namely, joy and happiness. Where joy is relational, happiness can be very solitary; where joy is everlasting, happiness is quite episodic and ephemeral; where joy both comes from and points back to the union of another eternal being, happiness is based on the enjoyment of things which are, by nature, finite. Think of related words like happen or happenstance—situations that come and go and upon which my happiness is based. When I see or taste or hear (fill in the blank), I am happy, but when that is gone, my happiness begins to fade as well. "On high the armies of the angels are giving praise. Here below, in the Church, the human choir takes up after them the same doxology. Above us, angels of fire make the thrice-holy hymn resound magnificently. Here below is raised the echo of their hymn. The festival of heaven's citizens is united with that of the inhabitants of earth in a single thanksgiving, a single upsurge of happiness, a single chorus of joy."[45]

Can you imagine being deep-down joyful with your spouse but having moments where you do not feel "happily married"? Or how many times has your joy as a parent been what carried you through those unhappy moments with your child? See, joy is an underlying

---

45 St. John Chrysostom (d. 407), *Homily On Isaiah* 4.1. Christopher Hall, *Worshipping with the Church Fathers* (Downer's Grove, IL: InterVarsity Academic, 2009), 69–70.

conviction of the presence of the other, while happiness comes and goes, contingent upon the circumstances of any given moment. In this way, we can imagine Jesus being joyful even going to Calvary, deeply aware of doing the Father's will, although one would be hard pressed to consider Him at all happy as He carries His cross.

St. Augustine offers us a sort of test to see if we are putting our life's energies into that which will bring joy or only that which causes temporary happiness. It is a very provocative examination of conscience for us: if we desire something *more before* we come to possess it, it is a temporal good, and one day the happiness it brings will have vanished and we shall be set upon looking for it (or its equivalent) yet again. However, if we desire something *more as* we have it, that is an eternal good—it's as if you just can't get enough of it—and that is the source of true joy.

> This, indeed, is the difference between temporal and eternal things, that something temporal is loved more before it is possessed, but loses its appeal when it comes along; this is because it cannot satisfy the soul, whose true and certain abode is eternity. But anything eternal is loved more fervently when acquired than when just desired. This is because while you were desiring it, you cannot possibly think better of it than it really is, so that it disappoints you when you find it does not come up to your expectations; on the contrary, however great your estimate of it while you are on the way to it, you will find it exceeded when you eventually attain to it.[46]

A temporal good is thus desired more before it is possessed, while the eternal good is desired more and more as it is possessed. The temporal good will always prove fleeting and can only disappoint if judged wrongly as something which will eternally satisfy. On the other hand, the eternal goods are always more and more delightful, as they prove inexhaustible with our appreciation, insight,

---

[46] St. Augustine, *On Christian Doctrine*, Book 1.38.42; trans. Edmund Hill, *Teaching Christianity: De Doctrina Christiana* (Hyde Park, NY: New City Press, 1996), 125.

and love only increasing as their infinite nature unfolds. For who gets tired of love or truth, bored with beauty, or who has grown indifferent to innocence?

Have your Christmases thus far in your life been valued as something only temporal? Can't we all relate to how the presents under the tree excite us for weeks, until they are opened and played with for a few hours?

What about joy among trials? How can we retain the joy the Holy Spirit infused into us at baptism as we make our way through this fallen world, so fraught with challenges and setbacks and injustices?

> Amma Syncletica said, "Great endeavors and hard struggles await those who are converted, but afterwards inexpressible joy. If you want to light a fire, you are troubled at first by smoke, and your eyes water. But in the end you achieve your aim." Now it is written: "Our God is a consuming fire." So we must light the divine fire in us with tears and struggle.[47]

> In him is my joy even if he chooses to send me some suffering, because I aspire to be purified as gold in the fire.[48]

---

47 *Sayings of the Desert Fathers*, Amma Syncletica, 2; Clément, *The Roots of Christian Mysticism*, 132. The *Sayings of the Desert Fathers* is a compilation mainly from the fifth-century of the aphorisms taught by the Christian ascetics, both male (*abba*) and female (*amma*), who spent their lives in the desert and hills of Egypt.

48 St. Gregory of Nazianzus, *Theological Poems*; Clément, *The Roots of Christian Mysticism*, 133.

> The Father of all things is a well-beloved kingdom. Anyone who is in him, anyone who establishes his dwelling in him, finds his joy in living as a stranger because he has for delicious food the beauty of God's face.[49]

The saints show us that joy is retained throughout tough times only when we are able to be still and find some kernel of gratitude for all God's labors for us. "In all circumstances give thanks, for this is the will of God for you in Christ Jesus" (1 Thess 5:18). *In all circumstances,* Paul says, not just the things we personally like or have chosen for ourselves. This does not mean we are grateful for the unemployment, the cancer, the divorce, or whatever other bad news comes our way. That would be unrealistic and an insult to our God-given desires. It does mean, however, that we remain faithful, trusting that consolation will return and that we are being asked to undergo a trial with purpose and even that joy of knowing that God will not abandon us.

What is the most spiritual pain you have experienced? Did you find God there? How?

What is your greatest fear? Is it the death of the person closest to you? What physical or material loss do you fear the most? Can you bring that moment to prayer and ask Jesus even now to be there, if or when that happens?

Do you tend to ascribe everything to God's will? Could you see how some events in your life are not directly caused by God but allowed for some other reason? Sin, for example, is not God's

49 Evagrius of Pontus, *Centuries,* Supplement, no. 57; Clément, *The Roots of Christian Mysticism,* 164.

will, but He allows it in order to honor our free will as well as to show us how much we need a sinless Savior. What else in your life has God allowed, bringing greater fruit out of it?

> This joy is not contrary to that grief, but from that grief it too is born. For he who grieves for his own faults, and confesses them, rejoices. Moreover, it is possible to grieve for our own sins, and yet to rejoice in Christ. Since then they were afflicted by their sufferings, for to you it is given not only to believe in him, but also to suffer for him Philippians 1:29, therefore he says, Rejoice in the Lord. For this can but mean, If you exhibit such a life that you may rejoice. Or when your communion with God is not hindered, rejoice. Or else the word in may stand for with: as if he had said, with the Lord. Always; again I will say, Rejoice. These are the words of one who brings comfort; as, for example, he who is in God rejoices always. Yea though he be afflicted, yea whatever he may suffer, such a man always rejoices. Hear what Luke says, that they returned from the presence of the Council, rejoicing that they were counted worthy to be scourged for His name. Acts 5:41 If scourging and bonds, which seem to be the most grievous of all things, bring forth joy, what else will be able to produce grief in us?[50]

So, we maintain joy, first, by giving God thanks, and, second, we retain joy in times of trial and deep disappointment by asking for Christ's own courage to keep moving on with life. "I have told you this so that you might have peace in me. In the world you will have trouble, but take courage, I have conquered the world" (Jn 16:33). A tried-and-true spiritual adage is never to make a decision when feeling desolate or disturbed, but to keep doing what you have been

---

50 St. John Chrysostom, *Homily on Philippians,* 14.1; Nicene and Post-Nicene Fathers edition: https://www.ccel.org/ccel/schaff/npnf113.iv.iii.xv.html, slightly adjusted.

doing, knowing that Jesus Himself has conquered anything that could take your (true) life. Such courage is not easy, and that is why it is Christ's own courage you seek, a courage in which He longs to give you a share. This is not natural bravery or, worse, foolhardy bravado—this is the courage of the martyr who lives first for Jesus and knows that in Him, everything else worth having will remain as well.

> His joy over our salvation, therefore, which was always in him inasmuch as he foreknew and predestined us, began to be in us when he called us (cf. Rom 8:29–30), and this joy, whereby we too shall be blessed, we rightly call ours, but this joy of ours grows and advances and through perseverance aims at its completion. It begins, therefore, in the faith of the reborn and is made complete in the reward of the resurrected. See, here is why I think it was said, *These things I have said to you, so that my joy may be in you and your joy may be complete—so that mine may be in you, and yours may be complete,* "for mine was always full even before you were called, when you were known by me as about to be called, but it also produced in you when you are formed into what I have foreknown of you. But yours will be complete because you will be blessed, which isn't yet the case, as you who didn't exist were created to be."[51]

So, although the Son of God has been Joy Itself forever, He now has become human so as to transmit that perfect Joy to each man and woman as much as possible. Joy is a communal reality, and the Joy of Christ longs to find its place in you also, as Augustine preaches.

Are you becoming more joyful, more loving, more at peace? If Jesus is true, these effects should be more and more detectable in your soul, in how you are with others. The doors to spiritual growth open only backward. You understand who you are becoming and who God has been for you not by planning out the future but by praying over the past—even the past twelve or twenty-four hours.

---

51 St. Augustine, *Tractate on the Gospel of John* §83.1; trans. Edmund Hill, *Homilies on the Gospel of John 41–124* (Hyde Park, NY: New City Press, 2020), 297–98.

This is why Israel tells its story over and over. The Jewish people are mainly responsible for consecrating the memory in that way, and in Advent, the Christians join them in seeing the long trek God has walked with His people. But now there is a new twist and destination in this pilgrimage of faith. The goal is no longer a building but a baby, no longer the Law but Love.

The Christian understanding of joy is also related to the gift of awe or wonder. Three hundred years before Christ, the Greek philosopher Aristotle (d. 322) wrote that all knowledge begins in wonder, whereas in the seventeenth century, the French philosopher Reneé Descartes (d. 1650) flipped that on its head and wrote that knowledge begins in doubt. Where are we today? Do most people in our society seek to know because they are in awe of what lies before them, or do they seek to know out of a cynical stance that there could ever be such a thing as truth?

This divergence remains more than a philosophical disagreement but characterizes two types of people in the world. Those who unknowingly follow the thought of Descartes go through life thinking their perspective determines reality. If I think this or that, this or that is the way things are. How terrifying to see the implications today of those who reject reality: the unborn, to some, are not only seen but treated as disposable parasites, a "cluster of cells" because that is what I think. Or how prevalent is the fiction that, regardless of my chromosomal makeup or physiology, if I think I am a man or a woman, or some other possibility, that is what I am, and no one else can penetrate my delusion.

Perhaps this is why the true meaning of Christmas is lost on so many. For true celebration is reserved for those who agree with how Aristotle (and, from him, most of the Christian tradition) sees the world: that is, there is a reality independent of my own opinion, and my job as a rational person is to conform my mind to what is. Of course, I am free to reject or ignore the objective world outside of myself, but I do that only to my self-imposed deception. At Christmas, then, we are to recognize a newborn child who will claim to be the Son of God. Either we kneel, or we turn away; adore, or avert our eyes.

This is no doubt why society is unwilling to go more deeply, to see how our larger secular celebrations are all really religious in origin. Perhaps we are uncomfortable receiving such a gift as God in the flesh and would rather stay on the surface level of gifts and glitter. But in a society where life has become cheap and the unborn are all too easily discarded, Christians need to reclaim the miracle of human life.

> You formed my inmost being; you knit me in my mother's womb. I praise you, because I am wonderfully made; wonderful are your works! My very self you know. My bones are not hidden from you, when I was being made in secret, fashioned in the depths of the earth. Your eyes saw me unformed; in your book all are written down; my days were shaped, before one came to be. How precious to me are your designs, O God; how vast the sum of them! Were I to count them, they would outnumber the sands; when I complete them, still you are with me. (Ps 139:13–18).

Do you ever find yourself in awe of an everyday reality—the fact that things exist, that you exist? Do you ever find yourself filled with gratitude for the life God has given you and has allowed you to live?

Are you fascinated by the way children are wide-eyed and amused by the simplest of things? Where have you retained some childlike wonder?

Does your Christian faith inform your political and societal views and actions as well? How do you stand up for the voiceless—for the unborn, the single mother, the outcast?

Obviously, wonder and a childlike simplicity go hand in hand. In his magisterial work *Orthodoxy*, the English wit and writer G. K. Chesterton (d. 1936) contrasted the modern scientist with the perennial child. He was bothered by how science reduces the patterns and predictabilities of nature to cold, inevitable laws, sapping the world of all its wonder. Repetition for the scientist, Chesterton saw, meant rote redundancy, but if we look at how the newest of human minds work, it is precisely in that repetition that wonder is found:

> Because children have abounding vitality, because they are in spirit fierce and free, therefore they want things repeated and unchanged. They always say, "Do it again"; and the grown-up person does it again until he is nearly dead. For grown-up people are not strong enough to exult in monotony. But perhaps God is strong enough to exult in monotony. It is possible that God says every morning, "Do it again" to the sun; and every evening, "Do it again" to the moon. It may not be automatic necessity that makes all daisies alike; it may be that God makes every daisy separately, but has never got tired of making them. It may be that He has the eternal appetite of infancy; for we have sinned and grown old, and our Father is younger than we.[52]

Is this not a perfect quote for an Advent-Christmas retreat? God the Father is "young" in that He cannot grow jaded or cynical. Our sins make us old, but the freshness of the Father's eternal birth of the Son is now ours in time: it is here in Bethlehem that we can reclaim our youth, our wonder, our innocence. "I extol you, I praise your name; for you have carried out your wonderful plans of old,

---

[52] G. K. Chesterton, *Orthodoxy*, ch. IV, "The Ethics of Elfland" (New York: Dodd, Mead, and Co. [1908] 1950), 108–9.

faithful and true" (Is 25:1). This is what Advent is preparing us for: the festivity of knowing that God is faithful and that His plan of old, what Isaiah and John the Baptist have been telling us, is finally being realized. We shall soon gather not only to feast and to sing, but even more deeply, and for those who do not enjoy the gifts of community, to see in that creche the consummation of God's plan and to behold the God who, for each of us, has become a newborn child.

> Bless the Lord, my soul! Lord, my God, you are great indeed! You are clothed with majesty and splendor, robed in light as with a cloak. You spread out the heavens like a tent; setting the beams of your chambers upon the waters. You make the clouds your chariot; traveling on the wings of the wind. You make the winds your messengers; flaming fire, your ministers. You fixed the earth on its foundation, so it can never be shaken. The deeps covered it like a garment; above the mountains stood the waters. At your rebuke they took flight; at the sound of your thunder they fled. They rushed up the mountains, down the valleys to the place you had fixed for them. You set a limit they cannot pass; never again will they cover the earth. You made springs flow in wadies that wind among the mountains. They give drink to every beast of the field; here wild asses quench their thirst. Beside them the birds of heaven nest; among the branches they sing. You water the mountains from your chambers; from the fruit of your labor the earth abounds. You make the grass grow for the cattle and plants for people's work to bring forth food from the earth, wine to gladden their hearts, oil to make their faces shine, and bread to sustain the human heart. . . . How varied are your works, Lord! In wisdom you have made them all; the earth is full of your creatures. (Ps 104:1–15, 24)

Christian anthropology differs greatly from how the world understands the nature and purpose of the human person. For the Christian, we have a sense of identity—to come to know who we are—in order that we may make ourselves a gift for others. Jesus knows who He is because He knows He is loved by the Father.

"This is my beloved Son, with whom I am well pleased" (Mt 17:5). Jesus knows who He is because He knows He has come from the Father and is going back to the Father.

This is the lesson He receives from the Father, the First who is fullness and who is the primary gift of self, the Begetter who hands Himself over eternally and fully to His Begotten Son in the unity of the Holy Spirit. "For just as the Father has life in himself, so also he gave to his Son the possession of life in himself" (Jn 5:26). This is the timeless donation of self the Son of God has eternally known and has received, and that is precisely how He lives His life incarnate in us: "For the Father himself loves you, because you have loved me and have come to believe that I came from God. I came from the Father and have come into the world. Now I am leaving the world and going back to the Father" (Jn 16:27–28). So as not to steal this gift of self away from us, on the night before He dies, Jesus sacramentally shows and liturgically establishes for us this movement from self-possession to self-gift. "This is my body," as if to say, *This is who I am; I know who I am and I freely stand before you and give my life for you.*

"This is my body . . . given for you." Now the time has come that you witness my total self-gift, this outpouring of humanity, of divinity, of love. "This is why the Father loves me, because I lay down my life in order to take it up again. No one takes it from me, but I lay it down on my own. I have power to lay it down, and power to take it up again. This command I have received from my Father" (Jn 10:17–18). This is the heart of the Eucharist: the Lord not only showing us who He is but willingly entering the souls of sinners in order to elevate us into His own belovedness. This is the Eucharist, and this is what you, too, are to become.

Even on a natural level, is this not what we wait for in everyone? We want each child to know that he or she is beloved, valued, seen, and safe. This is who you are—the son, the daughter, the friend. Yet we also work with them to see that they are not the center of reality, and their full maturity will come when they begin to live for others—when they no longer have to be told to do this or that chore, when they no longer do what is right only in order to be rewarded, and so on.

John the Baptist knows who he is and why he has come into the world: "I am the voice of one crying in the wilderness. . . . Make straight the way of the Lord" (Jn 1:23). His self-awareness is rooted in the most fundamental of truths, a humble, mortal creature before a perfect God. John knows he didn't create himself, and after years of living as a hermit (one who purposefully and prayerfully dwells in a desert setting), he understands how fragile even the most basic of life's necessities truly are. When pressed about his self-identity, he shuns any boasting or self-aggrandizement but instead draws from his meekness to announce, "Among you stands One whom you do not know, even he who comes after me, the thong of whose sandal I am not worthy to untie" (Jn 1:27).

Where and by whom do you feel most loved? Why? What is it about that love that makes it real? With whom do you feel most alive?

Do you tend to doubt people's love for you? Are there hurts still unhealed in your heart? Do you ever doubt God's perfect and unconditional love?

Is it this love that gives you your deepest sense of self? If not, from where do you derive your self-identity—human attention, riches, status, sex, physical appearance, etc.?

The baptism John offers is a Jewish cleansing, not the Christian sacrament. He is not the Way, but he is preparing the way. Religions of all sorts have such rites of purification as John displays in his ministry. But by descending into the waters and arising only to hear how he is the Father's beloved Son (cf. Mt 3:17; Mk 9:7; Lk 9:35), Jesus initiates a new baptism, one resulting not just in the healing of original sin and the cancellation of all actual sins (if any), but in the indwelling of the Holy Spirit.

It is fitting to think about baptism during Advent. Both stress the unmerited and undeserved gift of God. God longs to come to us; He waits for neither intellectual sophistication nor moral perfection. Both Advent and the sacrament of Baptism highlight the beauty of littleness and simplicity as well, as both hinge on the fact that a child is born unto us and this child is in need of care and tenderness.

A great prophet will be born to an elderly woman, God to a virgin, and both will come from a place too small to be of any significance, the paradox of the divine design. Both baptism and Advent stress the role of the family in transmitting the Faith. The fact that God Himself freely chose to be born into a family, wholly dependent for nine months on a mother and still for years to come dependent as well on a foster father, consecrates the daily and mundane relations (which we often take for granted, and more often fail to think of as "holy") within our own homes.

This is why your baptism was more of a rite of adoption than anything else. At that moment, God Himself chose to dwell in your soul as He invited you to dwell in Him, thereby elevating you from a creature into a child. While we rightly profess Jesus as the "only begotten Son of God" because Jesus is naturally one ("consubstantial") with the Father, we are made one through the gift and grace of incorporation. He is Son by an eternal birth ("begotten before all ages"); we are sons and daughters through sacramental rites of adoption—He Son by nature, we by grace. To realize this fully, we must own the reality of being baptized, no longer part of the world—dead to sin—and now claimed as Christ's own brothers and sisters.

St. Paul knew that this baptism was first a death to the world—a threefold immersion symbolizing the three days of Christ in the tomb, a threefold rising from that water symbolizing the resurrection. "Or are you unaware that we who were baptized into Christ Jesus were baptized into his death? We were indeed buried with him through baptism into death, so that, just as Christ was raised from the dead by the glory of the Father, we too might live in newness of life. For if we have grown into union with him through a death like his, we shall also be united with him in the resurrection" (Rom 6:2–5). "Christ has flooded the universe with divine and sanctifying waves. For the thirsty he sends a spring of living water from the wound which the spear opened in his side. From the wound in Christ's side has come forth the Church, and he has made her his Bride."[53] "Sanctify this water, that those who are baptized in it may be crucified with Christ, die with him, be buried with him, and rise again through adoption."[54]

What does it mean for you to die to sin? What might that practically look like—that is, what in your normal day would you have to put to death—an inordinate attachment to food, to social media, to drink, to lust, to always having to buy the best or highest-priced option, do you have to die to pride and a need to look better than others, etc.?

53 Origen (d. c. 253), *Commentary on the Psalms*, 77.31; Clément, *The Roots of Christian Mysticism*, 95.

54 *Apostolic Constitutions*, 7.43; Clément, *The Roots of Christian Mysticism*, 103. The *Apostolic Constitutions*, 8 books in all, come from mid-fourth-century Syria and deal mainly with Church conduct—Church leadership, how to organize a diocese and parish, how to celebrate liturgical rites, how to conduct oneself worthily of Christ while in the world, and so on.

What does union with God look like for you? In what areas have you freely kept Him away, and where might you still need to invite Him?

> When I think of the profusion of the names of the Spirit I am seized with dread: Spirit of God, Spirit of Christ, Spirit of Adoption. He renews us in baptism and resurrection. He blows where he wills. Source of light and life, he makes of me a temple, he makes me divine. . . . Everything that God does is done by the Spirit. He multiplies himself in tongues of fire and he multiplies his gifts, he raises up preachers, apostles, prophets, pastors, teachers. . . . He is another Comforter . . . as if he were another God.[55]

Do you renew your baptismal commitment to God every time you place your hand in the holy water font at Mass and make the Sign of the Cross? Could you use holy water at home and to bless those there?

> By the baptism of regeneration grace confers two benefits on us, one of which infinitely surpasses the other. It gives the first immediately, for in the water itself it renews us and causes the image of God to shine in us. . . . As for the other, it awaits our collaboration to produce it: it is the likeness of God. When our spirit begins to experience the deep sensation of savoring the goodness of the Holy Spirit, then we should know that grace

---

55 St. Gregory of Nazianzus, *Fifth Theological Oration* 29; Clément, *The Roots of Christian Mysticism*, 73.

> is beginning to overpaint the image with the likeness. Painters begin by sketching the outline of a portrait in a single color, then they gradually add the luster of one color to the other until they copy their model, right down to the very hairs of its head. In just such a way, the grace of God in baptism begins by making the image once again what it was when man first came into existence. Then when grace sees us aspiring with our whole will to the beauty of the likeness, and standing naked and at peace in his studio, then he adds the luster of one virtue after another, and, by raising the soul's beauty from splendor to splendor, makes it an unmistakable likeness. Our spiritual sensitivity shows us that we are in the process of being formed to the likeness. But we shall know its perfection only by illumination. . . . Indeed no one can attain to spiritual love unless he is brought to certainty by the light of the Holy Spirit. . . . And only the enlightenment of love, when it is added, shows that the image has completely attained the beauty of the likeness.[56]

Here we see a fairly early understanding about the difference between what shall later be called operative and cooperative grace. That is, as one comes to the font of baptism, one has nothing of meritorious value in his or her soul. It's not a very popular image in today's therapeutic world, but before baptism, we are rebels before God, depraved and spoiled children who have freely turned away from the One who has created all. That is why we cannot baptize ourselves but must be presented to another. It is a gift; it is the beginning of what we can start to partake of ourselves.

That is why Diadochus talks about a lesser gift, the gift of operative grace, where we find ourselves undergoing the gently physician's hand aimed at healing the wounds of original sin. Here we have nothing to offer, nothing of real value; we simply have to be still and let the healer go to work. Thereafter, however (in Diadochus's words), God can "await our collaboration to produce" the holiness He alone can offer. He does this through our free "yes," our response

---

[56] Diadochus of Photike (d. c. 500), *Gnostic Chapters* §89; Clément, *The Roots of Christian Mysticism*, 90–91.

to a gift that is never forced upon us. This is now cooperative grace, where the divine and human collaborate together to bring the latter into the fullness of what it has been created to be. This final state is the fullness of humanity when we most truly become like God Himself.

John was so on fire for the Lord, people actually wondered whether or not he was the Christ. "Now the people were filled with expectation, and all were asking in their hearts whether John might be the Messiah" (Lk 3:15). This is the goal of the entire Christian life: to be so one with Jesus that we begin to live His life as He lives ours—resembling Him in how we think and act and speak and desire. Does this mean we sell everything, take on some lifelong fast, renouncing the world in all its forms as John once did? Perhaps for some, but probably not you. You are probably being called right now to assess your life as it is and not being called to make some major life change. Be that as it may, any disciple of Jesus is always reviewing and reforming his or her life—daily prayer, monthly confession, annual retreat.

Instead, when asked what the people should do, they hear John tell them nothing they would not have already discerned in the Law:

> And the crowds asked him, "What then should we do?" He said to them in reply, "Whoever has two tunics should share with the person who has none. And whoever has food should do likewise." Even tax collectors came to be baptized and they said to him, "Teacher, what should we do?" He answered them, "Stop collecting more than what is prescribed." Soldiers also asked him, "And what is it that we should do?" He told them, "Do not practice extortion, do not falsely accuse anyone, and be satisfied with your wages." (Lk 3:10–14)

So, how do we live out this ancient message today? We share with those less fortunate, with food and clothing singled out here. Do you not do that already at your local mission, at St. Vincent de Paul, or Goodwill? John tells us not to cheat others, not to speak unjustly about anyone, and to be satisfied with the life God has given us. In other words, keep doing what you are doing, honestly select any place in your life where you know you are sinning, and offer that back to God through confession and firm amendment of resolve to love better.

In many ways, the season of Advent is like preparing to relocate in a big move: we go through what we need and box it up and discard that which we no longer use. Perhaps you could take inventory of your soul and list, on one column, those places you feel fruitful and responsible in the Father's hands—ready to hold His Son come Christmas—and, in the other column, mark down (at least mentally, if nothing else) those areas or activities where you know you are being secretive, selfish, and sinful.

During this third week of Advent, making our way to Christmas, we may also hear of the genealogies of Jesus Christ, immersing us yet again into His historical Jewish roots. These listings of names are not the stuff great sermons are made of—baldly factual, somewhat boring, or at least foreign, with all those unrecognizable names—but something important must be contained here, or else the Holy Spirit would not have given it to the Gospel authors.

St. Luke chronicles seventy-seven generations, while St. Matthew limits his list to three groups of fourteen generations, forty-two in all. Remember how different these two apostles were. Luke was a learned physician, someone who had studied for years and was steeped in Hellenic culture, a physician by trade and historian by avocation, one oriented more outward looking than the other Gospel writers (Matthew and Mark being more inward looking, and John certainly being upward looking, giving us the theologically loftiest of the Gospels).

Luke, therefore, does not emphasize how Jesus was of King David's line and does not begin with the Jewish "Father in faith," Abraham, but reaches all the way back to the first Adam, thereby stressing Christ's new universal messianic presence as the New Head of the human race. The number seventy-seven also reminds us of how often we must forgive (cf. Lk 17:4), and, according to St. Augustine, seven repeated teaches us that all persons are made in the image and likeness of God. How so? There are three persons of the Trinity who dwell in the sanctified soul, and since the body is made up of the four elements—earth, water, air, and fire—three plus four equals seven. This may be fanciful, but there is nothing in Sacred Scripture the Church Fathers do not seek to mine and find nuggets of truth and teaching.[57]

Matthew, we know, was a Jewish man who had been corralled into working for the Romans, collecting their taxes. We can easily imagine him as somewhat devout but someone inordinately attached to riches and the allure of making money despite the cost, socially or religiously. Christ, however, saw something else in this child of Abraham (cf. Mt 9:9–13) and calls him. In return, Matthew assiduously documents the major scenes of Christ's life, giving us the lengthiest of the four Gospels.

Being Jewish, Matthew stresses Jesus's lineage in terms of the line of the great patriarchs and kings of the Scriptures. Jesus is thus portrayed in terms of forty-two generations, the number of desert encampments the Jewish people had as Yahweh led them from the promised land (all listed throughout the Torah), Jesus here presented as the new Moses.

> But it is of no avail to say that our Lord, the Son of the blessed Virgin Mary, was true and perfect man, if He is not believed to be Man of that stock which is attributed to Him in the Gospel. For Matthew says, *The book of the generation of*

---

57 Cf. St. Augustine, *Sermon* 51.34.

Jesus Christ, the son of David, the son of Abraham (Mt 1:1), and follows the order of His human origin, so as to bring the lines of His ancestry down to Joseph to whom the Lord's mother was espoused. Whereas Luke going backwards step by step traces His succession to the first of the human race himself, to show that the first Adam and the last Adam were of the same nature. No doubt the Almighty Son of God could have appeared for the purpose of teaching, and justifying men in exactly the same way that He appeared both to patriarchs and prophets in the semblance of flesh; for instance, when He engaged in a struggle, and entered into conversation (with Jacob), or when He refused not hospitable entertainment, and even partook of the food set before Him. But these appearances were indications of that Man whose reality it was announced by mystic predictions would be assumed from the stock of preceding patriarchs. And the fulfilment of the mystery of our atonement, which was ordained from all eternity, was not assisted by any figures because the Holy Spirit had not yet come upon the Virgin, and the power of the Most High had not over-shadowed her: so that Wisdom building herself a house within her undefiled body, the Word became flesh; and the form of God and the form of a slave coming together into one person, the Creator of times was born in time; and He Himself through whom all things were made, was brought forth in the midst of all things. For if the New Man had not been made in the likeness of sinful flesh, and taken on Him our old nature, and being consubstantial with the Father, had deigned to be consubstantial with His mother also, and being alone free from sin, had united our nature to Him the whole human race would be held in bondage beneath the Devil's yoke, and we should not be able to make use of the Conqueror's victory, if it had been won outside our nature.

From the union of the two natures flows the grace of baptism. He makes a direct appeal to Empress Pulcheria for her help. But from Christ's marvelous sharing of the two natures, the mystery of regeneration shone upon us that through the self-same spirit, through whom Christ was conceived and born, we too, who were born through the desire of the flesh,

> might be born again from a spiritual source: and consequently, the Evangelist speaks of believers as those who were *born not of bloods, nor of the will of the flesh, nor of the will of man, but of God* (Jn 1:13).[58]

> The time had come when, having redeemed the world through his blood, he was to be acknowledged as king not of the house of David alone, but also of the whole Church; moreover, that he was maker and governor of all generations. Hence the angel properly said afterwards: "and the Lord God will give him the seat of David his father," and he immediately added, "and he will reign in the house of Jacob forever." Now, the house of Jacob refers to the universal Church, which through her faith in and confession of Christ pertains to the heritage of patriarchs—either among those who took their physical origin from the stock of the patriarchs or from among those who, though brought forth with respect to the flesh from other countries, were reborn in Christ by a spiritual washing.[59]

The genealogy is important for two reasons: the first is to look back and to ground Christ's person in real human history, and the second is to look forward to show that one's desire to belong to Christ no longer depends on this past lineage. Whereas the first covenanted people were determined by genes and geography, the new covenant is determined by gift and grace. Who among us does not appreciate knowing from where we come—the names and the stories of those who migrated to where we now live, what they did for a living, and any other more "colorful" anecdotes their life stories bring?

Unlike other Mediterranean religions of its day, Judaism began in an actual place at an actual time with an actual, historical person: "Abram was seventy-five years old when he set out from Harran"

---

[58] Pope Leo the Great, *Letter* 31.2–3, New Advent translation: https://www.newadvent.org/fathers/3604031.htm, slightly adjusted.

[59] The Venerable Bede (d. 735), *Homilies on the Gospels* 1.3; trans. Thomas C. Oden, *Luke: Volume 3 in the Ancient Christian Commentary on Scripture* (Downer's Grove, IL: InterVarsity Press, 2014), 17.

(Gn 12:4). Other religions of the day start their sacred stories in a more nebulous tone, for example, "In that time . . ." and then went on to offer fanciful tales of the gods and goddesses at war, at rest, erotically involved, dining, and dying. The genealogies of myths are full not only of familiar Greek and Roman deities but of natural objects and powers and forces as well (e.g., when Plato gives a genealogy for romantic love, he traces it back to the mingling of the forces of Poverty and of Fullness).

This is why St. Paul instructs young Timothy so: "I repeat the request I made of you when I was on my way to Macedonia, that you stay in Ephesus to instruct certain people not to teach false doctrines or to concern themselves with myths and endless genealogies, which promote speculations rather than the plan of God that is to be received by faith" (1 Tm 1:3–4). The entire point of Advent is to see that our humanity is rooted in a God who has come to earth at a particular time to a particular people in a very particular way—and, if this story is true, it is ultimately true; if not, nothing really matters for too long. But the apostles, the martyrs, the saints, and the best philosophers have all attested with their lives that this is no mere myth or fanciful fable but an invitation to know the one true God.

Look over photographs of family and friends and offer a prayer for them. Take some time to thank God for the way He has brought you into being, into this family, into this century, and country. The fact that your grandparents, your parents, and so on actually met and fell in love, and that someone cared more about you than themselves to bring you into this world, is nothing short of miraculous. What is your story?

Is there anyone in your genealogy who embarrasses you? How do you think Jesus looked upon His family line and saw adulterers, murderers, and all sorts of sinful people? Offer a prayer for your grandparents, parents, and godparents.

What sort of example of holiness do you strive to leave the younger generation in your life? Do you strive to set a model of proper piety, of active works of mercy, and love of neighbor?

Extended Prayer Period: A major component of Advent is coming to terms with the fact that we are saved by a vulnerable, helpless child. Christianity alone is the religion of the everyday, the simple, the ordinary, and the little way. The story Jesus refers to in Luke 4 shows us how God used the Jewish people to prepare the human race to understand that He desired to come to them in a very simple and straightforward way. Perhaps God's people got too used to the powerful pyrotechnics He could perform—the parting of the Red Sea, the destruction of a much bigger army, and so on—and the Lord decided now was the time to show them how love is actually stronger than power. Jesus said to the people in the synagogue at Nazareth: "Amen, I say to you, no prophet is accepted in his own native place. . . . Again, there were many lepers in Israel during the time of Elisha the prophet; yet not one of them was cleansed, but only Naaman the Syrian" (Lk 4:24, 27).

Take some time now to reflect on this story from 2 Kings. It recalls the story of Naaman, who is asked to find God in a very ordinary way, in a very insignificant spot on earth. Is this not the way God chooses to meet us most of the time—in our everyday life, in the car, at our workplace, in the friends and family He has put into our life?

Naaman, the army commander of the king of Aram, was highly esteemed and respected by his master, for through him the Lord had brought victory to Aram. But valiant as he was, the man was a leper. Now the Arameans had captured from the land of Israel in a raid a little girl, who became the servant of Naaman's wife. She said to her mistress, "If only my master would present himself to the prophet in Samaria! He would cure him of his leprosy." Naaman went and told his master, "This is what the girl from the land of Israel said." The king of Aram said, "Go. I will send along a letter to the king of Israel." So Naaman set out, taking along ten silver talents, six thousand gold pieces, and ten festal garments. He brought the king of Israel the letter, which read: "With this letter I am sending my servant Naaman to you, that you may cure him of his leprosy." When he read the letter, the king of Israel tore his garments and exclaimed: "Am I a god with power over life and death, that this man should send someone for me to cure him of leprosy? Take note! You can see he is only looking for a quarrel with me!" When Elisha, the man of God, heard that the king of Israel had torn his garments, he sent word to the king: "Why have you torn your garments? Let him come to me and find out that there is a prophet in Israel."

Naaman came with his horses and chariot and stopped at the door of Elisha's house.

Elisha sent him the message: "Go and wash seven times in the Jordan, and your flesh will heal, and you will be clean." But Naaman went away angry, saying, "I thought that he would surely come out to me and stand there to call on the name of the Lord his God, and would move his hand over the place, and thus cure the leprous spot. Are not the rivers of Damascus, the Abana and the Pharpar, better than all the waters of Israel? Could I not wash in them and be cleansed?" With this, he turned about in anger and left.

But his servants came up and reasoned with him: "My father, if the prophet told you to do something extraordinary, would you not do it? All the more since he told you, 'Wash, and be clean'?" So Naaman went down and plunged into the

> Jordan seven times, according to the word of the man of God. His flesh became again like the flesh of a little child, and he was clean. He returned with his whole retinue to the man of God. On his arrival he stood before him and said, "Now I know that there is no God in all the earth, except in Israel. Please accept a gift from your servant." (2 Kgs 5:1–15)

Naaman, the great king, was a leper. Do you sometimes feel this way, in charge and put together, but with spots in your life that make you feel less than whole? Where do you seek cleansing as Christmas approaches?

Do you tend to relegate God to the otherworldly, the "religious," or the ceremonial only? If so, do you think you have missed how God is acting or whom He has sent to reveal His presence to you?

What does it mean for you to find God in the everyday of your experience? Can you pray now to ask Him for the grace to have your understanding of Him expanded and your ability to find Him widened?

Are you God's because of His love or His power? Do you tend to see God more in rules or in relationships?

O God, who see how Your people faithfully await the feast of the Lord's Nativity, enable us, we pray, to attain the joys of so great a salvation and to celebrate them always with solemn worship and glad rejoicing. Though our Lord Jesus Christ, Your Son, who lives and reigns with You in the unity of the Holy Spirit, God for ever and ever. Amen.

Week 4

The Love of Advent

To be prayed from the first Sunday of Advent until Christmas Eve

℣. The Angel of the Lord brought tidings unto Mary
℟. And she conceived by the Holy Spirit.

Let us pray.

Pour forth we beseech Thee, O Lord, Thy grace into our hearts, that we to whom the Incarnation of Christ, Thy Son, was made known by the message of an Angel, may, by his Passion and Cross, be brought to the glory of his Resurrection. Through the same Christ, our Lord.
℟. Amen.

John the Baptist came into the world in a miraculous way. Beyond childbearing years, Elizabeth and Zechariah had to trust that God would use their old age to bring about new life, just as Mary would have to believe that her virginity could be fruitful. These are very "earthy" realities, and that is exactly how God has chosen to come to us—in our own particular life circumstances, in the conception of a baby, and in the fragility of maturing in this dangerous world.

This week, we light the fourth advent candle, representing the greatest gift of charity. Love and light are complementary in so many ways—illumination of what is really important, the warmth of closeness, that which lifts us out of the doldrums of darkness. Take some time to contemplate the beauty of light. It opens our eyes and allows us to see; it can warm us and often comfort us, especially in the midst of profound darkness.

What "lights" do you most often follow? Is it the Gospel or the news cycle?

What is the "darkness" in your world right now? Ask Christ, the Light, to enter there this season.

The fourth week of Advent is filled with messianic titles found in the Old Testament for Christ, liturgically placed and used here since at least the sixth century. From December 17 to 23, the "O Antiphons" are proclaimed liturgically for the seven final days leading up to the Nativity of Jesus:

Mt 1:18–24 (Year A)
Lk 1:26–38 (Year B)
Lk 1:39–45 (Year C)

An antiphon is traditionally a biblical verse proclaimed liturgically, and these seven are all messianic proclamations from the Old Testament. These are fitting cries from the heart, beginning with the pleading "O" and then invoking a messianic title for Jesus—securely rooting the fourth week of Advent into the story of Israel—and then invoking the One who is to come to work a great wonder for the sake of His people. In order, then, these ancient antiphons are:

> *O Sapientia* (December 17: Sir 24:3), meaning, "O Wisdom," as we pray: "O Wisdom of our God Most High, guiding creation with power and love: come to teach us the path of knowledge!"
>
> *O Adonai* (December 18: Ex 3:14), meaning, "O Lord, O Ruler," as we pray: "O Leader of the House of Israel, giver of the Law to Moses on Sinai: come to rescue us with your mighty power!"
>
> *O Radix Jesse* (December 19: Is 11:1), meaning, "O Root of Jesse," as we pray: "O Root of Jesse's stem, sign of God's love for all his people: come to save us without delay!"
>
> *O Clavis David* (December 20: Is 22:22; Rv 3:7), meaning, "O Key of David," as we pray: "O Key of David, opening the gates of God's eternal kingdom: come and free the prisoners of darkness."
>
> *O Oriens* (December 21: Jer 23:5; Zec 3:8, 6:12), meaning, "O Rising Dawn" or "Morning Star," as we pray: "O Radiant Dawn, splendor of eternal light, sun of justice: come and shine on those who dwell in darkness and in the shadow of death."
>
> *O Rex Gentium* (December 22: Jer 10:7; Hag 2:7), meaning, "O King of the Nations," as we pray: "O King of all nations and keystone of the Church: come and save man, whom you formed from the dust!"
>
> *O Emmanuel* (December 23: Is 7:14, 8:8; Lk 1:31–33), meaning, "God is with us," as we pray: "O Emmanuel, our King and Giver of Law: come to save us, Lord our God!"

As mentioned in week 1, you may recognize these titles from the hymn for Advent, "O come, O come, Emmanuel." This hymn is originally an eighth-century plainchant centered around the O Antiphons as we still have them today. Granted, it may have been a long while since your freshman Latin course, but if you took the first letter of each of these ancient titles, as these monks did, you would get S-A-R-C O-R-E which, when inverted, reads ERO CRAS. The words *ero cras* make up a Latin acrostic meaning, "I shall be present (*ero*) tomorrow (*cras*)."

The Church decorates these seven days with such flourish because we are being readied to meet the One for whom all ages have awaited: "But blessed are your eyes, because they see, and your ears, because they hear. Amen, I say to you, many prophets and righteous people longed to see what you see but did not see it, and to hear what you hear but did not hear it" (Mt 13:16–17). The *O Antiphons* mount the expectations as we move from the more abstract titles of "Wisdom," "Rule," "Root," and "Key" into the more intimate and embraceable images of "King" and a "God with us."

During this fourth week of Advent, the Church will also pray with a new Preface at Mass. The Preface for weeks 1–3 has now served its purpose. Whereas we prayed in Preface I for weeks now about "watching" for the "great promise" for which "we now dare to hope," which is now becoming a visible reality. Therefore, the Church now prays:

> It is truly right and just, our duty and our salvation, always and everywhere to give you thanks, Lord, holy Father, almighty and eternal God, through Christ our Lord. For all the oracles of the prophets foretold him, the Virgin Mother longed for him with love beyond all telling, John the Baptist sang of his coming and proclaimed his presence when he came. It is by his gift that already we rejoice at the mystery of his Nativity, so that he may find us watchful in prayer and exultant in his praise. And so, with Angels and Archangels, with Thrones and Dominions, and with all the hosts and Powers of heaven, we sing the hymn of your glory, as without end we acclaim: Holy, Holy, Holy . . .

Think of the obstacles the Son of God had to overcome to enter this world—a virgin mother possibly misunderstood for a time by her doting fiancé, a land torn asunder by political and religious divides, a people who were clearly unwilling to accept that the Messiah was not a political revolutionary but one insistent on love of enemy, and so on. Why do you think God tends to use such obstacles, shortcomings, and often even our own mistakes to work His greatest power (think of the Cross, if nothing else)? How does insecurity, loneliness, and even your own sinfulness bring you out of yourself?

When you pray over the O Antiphons, do you have a favorite Old Testament title for Jesus? Overall, what is your favorite title or image for Jesus—Savior, Friend, Counselor, etc.? Why are you attracted to such a name for Him?

Do you imitate Mary in "longing for Jesus with love beyond all telling"? And, like John the Baptist, do you "proclaim his presence" in the way you live?

Depending on the liturgical year (A, B, or C), either the third or this fourth week of Advent will proclaim Lk 1:26–38, fittingly the Church's most announced Gospel—proclaiming it also on the solemnity of the Annunciation on March 25, it is the central message commemorating our Lady's Immaculate Conception on December 8, and it is the Gospel for Our Lady of Guadalupe on December 12.

> In the sixth month, the angel Gabriel was sent from God to a town of Galilee called Nazareth, to a virgin betrothed to a man named Joseph, of the house of David, and the virgin's name was Mary. And coming to her, he said, "Hail, favored

one! The Lord is with you." But she was greatly troubled at what was said and pondered what sort of greeting this might be. Then the angel said to her, "Do not be afraid, Mary, for you have found favor with God. Behold, you will conceive in your womb and bear a son, and you shall name him Jesus. He will be great and will be called Son of the Most High, and the Lord God will give him the throne of David his father, and he will rule over the house of Jacob forever, and of his kingdom there will be no end."

But Mary said to the angel, "How can this be, since I have no relations with a man?" And the angel said to her in reply, "The holy Spirit will come upon you, and the power of the Most High will overshadow you. Therefore the child to be born will be called holy, the Son of God. And behold, Elizabeth, your relative, has also conceived a son in her old age, and this is the sixth month for her who was called barren; for nothing will be impossible for God." Mary said, "Behold, I am the handmaid of the Lord. May it be done to me according to your word." Then the angel departed from her. (Lk 1:26–38)

Pray over the words and actions of this passage, as it is the central truth of the Christian Faith—through the fidelity of a woman, God Himself enters His own creation, writing Himself into the story of each our lives.

Why does God send an angel, a created messenger, and not simply come Himself through the Holy Spirit? What does that say about God's longing to share His life and desire to save the world through us?

What significance is there in Mary's being addressed personally by name? Do you trust God knows you through and through and is with you at every moment and in every thought? Are you able to sit for a time reflecting on the intimacy He desires from you?

How do you think Mary was troubled? What did she

ponder? Being sinless, there is obviously a way to "wrestle with God" that does not incur guilt. How do you speak to God about the tough questions of life?

Have you ever noticed the Holy Spirit's "overshadowing" Mary here is exactly what happens at every Mass? At the consecration, we witness the priest putting his hands over the bread and wine, "overshadowing" them (called the Epiclesis, the "calling down"), and what was once human and natural now becomes a divine person united to a human nature—the Body and Blood of Jesus—exactly what happened when the Son of God became a man in Mary's womb.

At this Good News, the angel points Mary toward Elizabeth. In your celebrations, to whom do you first go?

What does Mary mean by "Behold"? This is a word which means "Look at me." Do you allow God to see you, to know you, to behold you?

That the Lord then was manifestly coming to His own things, and was sustaining them by means of that creation which is supported by Himself, and was making a recapitulation of that disobedience which had occurred in connection with a tree, through the obedience which was exhibited by Himself when He hung upon a tree, the effects also of that deception being done away with, by which that virgin Eve, who was already espoused to a man, was unhappily misled—was happily announced, through means of the truth spoken by the angel to the Virgin Mary, who was also espoused to a man.

For just as the former was led astray by the word of an angel, so that she fled from God when she had transgressed His word; so did the latter, by an angelic communication, receive the glad tidings that she should bear God, being obedient to His word. And if the former did disobey God, yet the latter was persuaded to be obedient to God, in order that the Virgin Mary might become the Advocate of the virgin Eve. And thus,

> as the human race fell into bondage to death by means of a virgin, so is it rescued by a virgin; virginal disobedience having been balanced in the opposite scale by virginal obedience. For in the same way the sin of the first created man receives amendment by the correction of the First-begotten, and the coming of the serpent is conquered by the harmlessness of the dove, those bonds being unloosed by which we had been fast bound to death.[60]

St. Irenaeus of Lyons spent his life combating what we call today "Gnosticism," stemming from one of the Greek words for "knowledge." Anyone who is today labeled a Gnostic was someone who denied God could literally become man, in no way could the divine mingle truly with the material. St. John the Evangelist was one of the first to detect this heresy, and that is why in his letters he so strongly teaches about the very particular and concrete flesh of Jesus, God-made-man, even opening up his first letter with this absolute:

> What was from the beginning, what we have heard, what we have seen with our eyes, what we looked upon and touched with our hands concerns the Word of life—for the life was made visible; we have seen it and testify to it and proclaim to you the eternal life that was with the Father and was made visible to us—what we have seen and heard we proclaim now to you, so that you too may have fellowship with us; for our fellowship is with the Father and with his Son, Jesus Christ. We are writing this so that our joy may be complete. (1 Jn 1:1–4)

Notice how John casts community and true joy in light of accepting that Jesus is truly God and man. The Father chooses to reveal His fullness in the Son, and in coming to the Son, we not only come to the fullness of God but also to one another. This is the Church, the Mystical Body, which Jesus began to form on the Annunciation and which will soon be visible to all willing to see.

---

[60] St. Irenaeus of Lyons, *Against Heresies* 5.19.1, New Advent translation: https://www.newadvent.org/fathers/0103519.htm.

Like many Christians still today, the ancient Gnostics, however, remain "spiritual" but never "material." They praise a God who remains distant and ethereal, and therefore a "god" who can be easily made into their own image and likeness. Is this not the "spiritual but not religious" of today's generation—no commitment to what the Church has always taught, no obligation to worship if some other appointment takes precedent, no sense of sacred space or a holy season? If God and the ways of God are disappearing from modern culture, this is why: a "god" who remains aloof and apart, with no concrete commitments or even physical demands, will not only be manipulated for convenience's sake but will eventually be made obsolete.

Think of Irenaeus's words above. Imagine living in the second century with him—this newly founded religion of "The Way," Christianity, was spreading rather successfully and found itself having to combat the pagan mindset that there were two distinct worlds that would never meet: the spiritual and the divine versus the material and the human. But the bishop of Lyons tells a different story, starting with woman. Whereas Eve was seduced by a fallen angel, the New Eve, Mary, surrendered to the message of a faithful angel. From her comes a New Adam, a new head of the human race who has become one of us in order to gather us all into one. In this gathering, Jesus Christ continues His divine presence, and the ancient battle between God and the enemy wages until all are victorious. This is the Gospel summed up in one line, "I will put enmity between you and the woman, and between your offspring and hers; they will strike at your head, while you strike at their heel" (Gn 3:15). This verse is known as the *Protoevangelium*, or "the first gospel," in that it foreshadows all that Jesus and Mary and the entire Church will do against the devil.

> For the birth of Christ is the source of life for Christian folk, and the birthday of the Head is the birthday of the body. Although every individual that is called has his own order, and all the children of the Church are separated from one another by intervals of time, yet as the entire body of the faithful

being born in the font of baptism is crucified with Christ in His passion, raised again in His resurrection, and placed at the Father's right hand in His ascension, so with Him are they born in this nativity. For any believer in whatever part of the world that is re-born in Christ, quits the old paths of his original nature and passes into a new man by being re-born; and no longer is he reckoned of his earthly father's stock but among the seed of the Savior, Who became the Son of man in order that we might have the power to be the sons and daughters of God. For unless He came down to us in this humiliation, no one would reach His presence by any merits of his own.[61]

Do you understand how all of humanity was first "gathered" in our first parents, Adam and Eve, and how God "regathered" all of us again in Mary and Jesus?

What comes to mind when you think of Jesus's "gathering" all to Himself? Do you find this freeing? What is your role in this new mission?

What significance does Jesus's flesh have for you on a practical, daily level? Do you pray to love the Eucharist—Jesus Himself—more, and take time to make a visit at your local parish or sign up for weekly Eucharistic Adoration?

[61] Pope Leo the Great (d. 461), *Sermon* 26.2 (the 6th H*omily on the Nativity*), New Advent translation: https://www.newadvent.org/fathers/360326.htm; slightly adjusted.

Another error of early Christians was to so stress the divinity of Jesus Christ; they really never made room for His truly becoming human. In this way, divinity remained aloof and apart from the human race. Take Noetus, for example, who was at his heretical height around 230 in modern-day Turkey. Noetus gained popularity by explaining the Trinity in a very easy to grasp but very dangerous to hold position, which was later named "Modalism" or "Patripassianism." Early Christians did not always find it easy to understand how one God could simultaneously be also three Divine Persons and, by implication, how Jesus could be a separate Divine Person distinct from the Father.

Noetus's error was drastic, and for it, he was eventually excommunicated. The Trinity is like water, Noetus preached: just as water can take on three different forms—liquid, solid, and steam—God does the same. So, in fact, "Father," "Son," and "Holy Spirit" are only three different names for the one and the same God, not distinct persons, but only three different modes: in an early time, He revealed Himself as Father; in Jesus, He let Himself be known as Son, and now He comes to us as the Holy Spirit. Thus the name modalism, as well as the name patripassianism—as it is really the Father (*pater-*) under different guises, and so it is really He who suffers (*-passion*). Such materialistic imagery was easily understood by many but quickly condemned by the bishops.

Let's pray over a couple of sections by St. Hippolytus in Rome aimed against this heresy of Modalism, once again reaffirming that necessary connection between doctrine and devotion:

> There is only one God, brethren, and we learn about him only from sacred Scripture. It is therefore our duty to become acquainted with what Scripture proclaims and to investigate its teachings thoroughly. We should believe them in the sense that the Father wills, thinking of the Son in the way the Father wills, and accepting the teaching he wills to give us with regard to the Holy Spirit. Sacred Scripture is God's gift to us and it should be understood in the way that he intends: we should not do violence to it by interpreting it according to our own preconceived ideas.

God was all alone and nothing existed but himself when he determined to create the world. He thought of it, willed it, spoke the word and so made it. It came into being instantaneously, exactly as he had willed. It is enough then for us to be aware of a single fact: nothing is coeternal with God. Apart from God there was simply nothing else. Yet although he was alone, he was manifold because he lacked neither reason, wisdom, power, nor counsel. All things were in him and he himself was all. At a moment of his own choosing and in a manner determined by himself, God manifested his Word, and through him he made the whole universe.

When the Word was hidden within God himself he was invisible to the created world, but God made him visible. First God gave utterance to his voice, engendering light from light, and then he sent his own mind into the world as its Lord. Visible before to God alone and not to the world, God made him visible so that the world could be saved by seeing him. This mind that entered our world was made known as the Son of God. All things came into being through him; but he alone is begotten by the Father.

The Son gave us the law and the prophets, and he filled the prophets with the Holy Spirit to compel them to speak out. Inspired by the Father's power, they were to proclaim the Father's purpose and his will.

So the Word was made manifest, as Saint John declares when, summing up all the sayings of the prophets, he announces that this is the Word through whom the whole universe was made. He says: *In the beginning was the Word, and the Word was with God, and the Word was God. Through him all things came into being; not one thing was created without him.* And further on he adds: *The world was made through him, and yet the world did not know him. He entered his own creation, and his own did not receive him.*[62]

---

[62] Hippolytus of Rome (c. 170–c. 235), *Treatise Against the Heresy of Noetus*, §9–12; *Liturgy of the Hours*, *op. cit.*, 370–72.

Advent is the time to stay with the humanity of Jesus Christ. He comes from a particular historical lineage. He comes from heaven to receive all of humanity in the womb of His virgin mother. He is born at a particular time in a particular place to a particular people. He is a divine person who has now assumed to Himself the fullness of human nature, awaiting birth and a visible manifestation to all come Christmas Day.

In this fourth week of Advent, however, we are being prepared for two births, actually—of course, we are leading up to the birth of God, but we are also asked to stop and spend some time with the birth of John the Baptist. Because the conception of each of these lives was so extraordinary—a baby unto a couple well past childbearing years and one born unto a virgin—there is naturally a questioning wonder or even a type of fear that would accompany such an event.

Both Zechariah and Mary experience a sort of agitation, understandably, finding themselves before an angel (see Lk 1:12 and Lk 1:29). Gabriel initially understands sympathetically and assures them that they need not be afraid (cf. Lk 1:13 and Lk 1:30). Through the angelic pronouncement, God gives each of the boys their names—*John* at Lk 1:13 and *Jesus* at Lk 1:31, and both are assured to be "great" (Lk 1:15 and Lk 1:32). Zechariah, as well as Mary, question this rather extraordinary event (see Lk 1:18 and Lk 1:34), and despite their very different intentions and outcomes, both complete this even with a canticle of praise (see Lk 1:68–79 and Lk 1:46–55).

In Zechariah's case, he is struck dumb for doubting the angel Gabriel. "'Then Zechariah said to the angel, 'How shall I know this? For I am an old man, and my wife is advanced in years.' And the angel said to him in reply, 'I am Gabriel, who stand before God. I was sent to speak to you and to announce to you this good news. But now you will be speechless and unable to talk until the day these things take place, because you did not believe my words, which will be fulfilled at their proper time'" (Lk 1:18–20).

Zechariah initially fails to trust in God's ability to work wonders. Perhaps he doubts the angel is who he says he is, and that is why Gabriel explains his position before God: "I am Gabriel, who stand before God."

> The angel took away his speech,
> To frighten that investigator.
> If the high priest was punished
> Because he discussed and investigated in order to learn
> [About] the birth and conception
> Of the preacher and thing-made,
> [There is] shaking, fear, and terror
> If someone presumes to investigate
> The begetting of the Lord of all.
> Zechariah, because he discussed,
> His mouth was muzzled with silence.
> He then honored with silence
> What he had discussed.
> How much more should we honor with silence
> The begetting of the Firstborn?
> He who discusses the Child
> Of his womb is to be blamed.
> Let him be afraid, who approaches
> Essence, to investigate
> Its Beloved in its womb!
> Zechariah uncovered
> The truth about himself with his question.
> Likewise, everyone who
> Asks in any way,
> Shows by his question
> That he had not previously believed.[63]

The great Syrian poet Ephrem sees in Zechariah's incredulity a lack of faith, but he also recognizes how the merciful Messiah uses his unbelief to help Zechariah grow in self-awareness. God will use

---

63 Ephrem the Syrian, *Hymn 9* on Faith; trans. Jeffrey T. Wickes, *St. Ephrem the Syrian: Hymns on Faith* (Washington, DC: Catholic University of America Press, 2015), 117.

whatever He can, whatever we give Him, and here doubt becomes discovery.

Do you ever beat yourself up for not instantly believing God, for not instinctually following God? What has the Lord done with that?

When you look back at those years you were unfaithful, do you see how the Lord never really left you and how He has used those experiences for your own growth in His Spirit?

As we shall see, Mary, too, asks Gabriel how such a new life could take place. But Mary is not punished for her question. What's the difference? Perhaps Zechariah is not struck mute for his actual questioning but for the manner with which he demands divine proof. He was incredulous that such a feat could ever occur—"How shall I know?" In other words, "What proof can you give me that this is so?" That seems to be how the angel Gabriel interprets Zechariah's words, for he punishes him not for his question but for his lack of faith.

We can conclude this because Mary also inquires into Gabriel's message. But the difference seems that Mary does not demand a higher verification or a more certain confirmation; she asks because she simply wonders how this child's conception could take place. "And coming to her, Gabriel said, 'Hail, favored one! The Lord is with you.' But she was greatly troubled at what was said and pondered what sort of greeting this might be. Then the angel said to her, 'Do not be afraid, Mary, for you have found favor with God.'"

> The Church observes the birth of John as in some way sacred; and you won't find any other of the ancient worthies whose birth we officially celebrate. We celebrate John's, we also celebrate Christ's. This point cannot be passed over in silence, and if I may not perhaps be able to explain it in a manner that such an important matter deserves, it is still worth thinking about a little more deeply and fruitfully than usual.
>
> John is born of an old woman who is barren; Christ is born of a young woman who is a virgin. Barrenness gives birth to John, virginity to Christ. The normal and proper age of parents was lacking with the birth of John, no marital embrace occurred for the birth of Christ. The former is announced in the declaration of the angel, with the angel's annunciation the latter is conceived. That John will be born is not believed, and his father is struck dumb; that Christ will be born is believed, and he is conceived by faith. First of all faith makes its entry into the heart of the virgin, and there follows fruitfulness in the mother's womb.
>
> Zechariah is given a rebuke, she is given information. He is told, "because you didn't believe"; Mary is told, "Here is the answer to your question." They are almost the same words: *By what shall I know this?* and, *How shall this come about?* But the difference didn't escape the one who heard the words, and could see the heart. In the words of each the thoughts of each were hidden; hidden, though, from human beings, not from the angel; or rather, not hidden from the one who was speaking through the angel.
>
> Finally, John is born when the daylight begins to diminish, and the night begins to grow longer. Christ is born when the night begins to be curtailed, and the day begins to increase.[64]

Mary's fidelity in God's promise to be ever near sustained her through life and under the cross of her beloved Son. She trusted God not because she had an easy life, but because she knew He was life (cf. Jn 14:6), and anything apart from Him, however comfortable or "successful," would, in the end, only disappoint.

---

64 St. Augustine, *Sermon* 293.1 (preached 413); trans. Edmund Hill, O.P, *Sermons (273–305A)*, 148–49.

What is your most often asked question for God? Do you ask in trust or in frustration or in outright doubt of his goodness?

How should one confront God? Could you see a way of asking God about His plans for you without sounding arrogant or skeptical?

Do you have a relationship with your guardian angel (after all, Advent and Christmas are the time for angels)? "See that you do not despise one of these little ones, for I say to you that their angels in heaven always look upon the face of my heavenly Father" (Mt 18:10). Pray with your guardian angel, asking for a greater sense of trust in God's plans for you and to see better all the ways—angelic, human, and natural—that God seeks to console you.

Angel of God, my guardian dear,
to whom God's love commits me here,
ever this day, be at my side,
to light and guard, Rule and guide. Amen.

Mary emerges as the perfect disciple and model of Christian holiness. This is not so much for what she does, but for who she is—it is not her only bearing the Son of God, as awesome as that is, but it is mainly for her docile trust and filial piety before the Father. "While Jesus was speaking, a woman from the crowd called out and said to him, 'Blessed is the womb that carried you and the breasts at which you nursed.' He replied, 'Rather, blessed are those who hear the word of God and observe it'" (Lk 11:27–28).

It is not the body of Mary that makes her exemplar—that would be of the "old" way of knowing the divine, through one's family lineage. What makes Mary our Queen is that she never wavered in her love of God and man. In fact, her love was so immaculate that in her trust, God and man are made one in the presence of her Son Jesus Christ. Her *fiat*—let it be done—becomes the space where heaven and earth meet, where we must go if we are going to come to the true Christ, the fullness of God. Or as one fifth-century bishop put it:

> She who called us here today is the Holy Mary; the untarnished vessel of virginity; the spiritual paradise of the second Adam (cf. Rom 5:14; 1 Cor 15:21–22, 45–49); the workshop for the union of natures; the market-place of the contract of salvation; the bridal chamber in which the Word took the flesh in marriage; the living bush of human nature, which the fire of a divine birth-pang did not consume (Ex 3:2); the veritable swift cloud (Is 19:1) who carried in her body the one who rides upon the cherubim; the purest fleece (Jg 6:37–38) drenched with the rain which came down from heaven, whereby the shepherd clothed himself with the sheep (cf. Jn 10:11); handmaid and mother (cf. Lk 1:38, 43), virgin and heaven, the only bridge for God to mankind; the awesome loom of the divine economy upon which the robe (Jn 19:23) of union was ineffably woven. The loom-worker was the Holy Spirit; the wool-worker the overshadowing power from on high (Lk 1:35). The wool was the ancient fleece of Adam; the interlocking thread the spotless flesh of the Virgin. The weaver's shuttle was propelled by the immeasurable grace of him who wore the robe; the artisan was the Word who entered in through her sense of hearing.[65]

---

65 Proclus of Constantinople (d. 446), *Homily on the Theotókos* §1.1; trans., Maximos Constas, accessed at: https://www.pappaspatristicinstitute.com/post/proclus-of-constantinople-and-his-homily-on-the-theotokos-delivered-in-the-presence-of-nestorius. This homily was delivered in the presence of the heresiarch Nestorius who refused to invoke Mary as Mother of God (in Greek, *Theotókos*) and instead would call upon her only as the

Take some time to pray over these images for the Blessed Virgin Mary in her divine motherhood. Do any of these resonate with you, bringing greater affection for Our Lady?

- Vessel of Virginity, wholly God's alone
- Spiritual Paradise, the New Eve helping recreate reality
- Workshop of Union between Divinity and Humanity
- Market-Place for the contract between God and Man
- Bridal Chamber where God and Man wed
- The Unconsumed Bush
- The Body Who Carries God Himself
- Pure Fleece, covering God's tiny body
- Handmaid and Mother
- The Bridge between Heaven and Earth
- The Loom who weaves God into Man

John the voice and Jesus the Word are meant to be seen together in Advent. No one is born alone and apart from others. We are inevitably connected to not only our mother but a vast array of family as well. Notice all the similarities between these two. Both are, for instance, ushered in by a sacred song, a canticle. With the news of John's upcoming birth, Zechariah proclaims the *Benedictus,* Latin for its opening word "*Blessed* be the Lord" at Lk 1:68–79; while at the Annunciation, Mary sings her beloved *Magnificat,* from the opening verb of Lk 1:46–55, "My soul *proclaims* the greatness of the Lord." Priests and religious brothers and sisters are obligated to pray Morning and Evening Prayer (at least), and these two canticles play a central part in each of those prayer times.

The *Benedictus* or "The Canticle of Zechariah" is prayed in the morning because it foreshadows the beginning of the Christian revolution. An aged husband and wife have miraculously conceived a child whose entire life will be spent pointing to fulfillment of the

mother of Jesus, insisting that no woman could be mother to the Son of God but only to his human nature. Nestorius was condemned and excommunicated at the Council of Ephesus in 431.

human heart's deepest desires, the everlasting Messiah, the God-made-man.

Then Zechariah his father, filled with the holy Spirit, prophesied, saying:

> Blessed be the Lord, the God of Israel;
> he has come to his people and set them free.
> He has raised up for us a mighty savior,
> born of the house of his servant David.
> Through his holy prophets he promised of old
> that he would save us from our enemies,
> from the hands of all who hate us.
> He promised to show mercy to our fathers
> and to remember his holy covenant.
> This was the oath he swore to our father Abraham:
> to set us free from the hands of our enemies,
> free to worship him without fear,
> holy and righteous in his sight all the days of our life.
> You, my child, shall be called the prophet of the Most High;
> for you will go before the Lord to prepare his way,
> to give his people knowledge of salvation
> by the forgiveness of their sins.
> In the tender compassion of our God
> the dawn from on high shall break upon us,
> to shine on those who dwell in darkness and the shadow of death,
> and to guide our feet into the way of peace (Lk 1:68–79).
> Glory to the Father and to the Son and to the Holy Spirit,
> as it was in the beginning, is now, and will be forever. Amen.

What resonates most strongly with you as you pray these words?

From what "enemies" has the Lord saved you?

Have you shown gratitude for living in a land where you can worship God "without fear"?

How do you see your "knowledge of salvation" related to your "forgiveness of sins"?

Zechariah breaks into these words upon being freed from his angelically imposed silence. Struck dumb for doubting Gabriel's message, Zechariah's prophetic message to all of posterity is to remember who God really is. We all have to be constantly purified to remember that the God we think we have a grasp of is much more mysterious, much more merciful, much more loving than we have come to imagine. He is the God who saves us from our enemies and who wants us to know that He has saved us. We are saved. You are saved! This is what John the Baptist came to tell us, and these words begin in the one who helped bring him into the world, one whose skepticism has been consecrated into surety.

> Hear what Zechariah, prophesying and blessing God, said: "Blessed be the Lord God of Israel, for he has visited and redeemed his people." Notice in these words that Zechariah

> was telling by way of prophecy, as if it had already come to pass, what he had foreseen in spirit had begun and would soon come to pass. By his appearance in the flesh our Lord was visiting us when we were distancing ourselves from him, and he chose to seek out and justify us when we were sinners. He visited us as a doctor visits an ill patient, and, in order to cure the ingrained sickness of our pride, he gave us the example of his own humility. He redeemed his people by giving us freedom, at the price of his own blood—we who had been sold into the slavery of sin and were committed to serving the ancient enemy. Therefore the Apostle exhorts us, saying, "For you have been purchased at a great price. Glorify and carry God in your bodies" (1 Cor 6:20).[66]

While the Church prays with Zechariah in the morning, Mary's Magnificat is prayed every evening in homes and monasteries, priories and convents across the world because we can end each day resting in the promises God has now in fact achieved. We are living in the last day, in the age of Jesus Christ. There will be no more event that changes the course of history except for His final coming. In the meantime, the battle continues—the strong versus the weak, the proud against the humble, the mighty against the powerless, the rich exploiting the poor, and the hungry at the hands who have more than their fill. This baby was not going to be a normal child, but it was clear to His mother that the child to be born was going to bring about an upheaval of infinite significance. This social struggle is recast in the words of Mary, who sings about a revolution she knows has begun in her very womb:

> And Mary said:
> My soul proclaims the greatness of the Lord,
> my spirit rejoices in God my Savior,
> for he has looked with favor on his lowly servant.
> From this day all generations will call me blessed:

---

66 The Venerable Bede, *Homilies on the Gospel* 2.20, Commentary on Lk 1:68, accessed at: https://catenabible.com/lk/1.

the Almighty has done great things for me,
and holy is his Name.
He has mercy on those who fear him in every generation.
He has shown the strength of his arm,
he has scattered the proud in their conceit.
He has cast down the mighty from their thrones,
and has lifted up the lowly.
He has filled the hungry with good things,
and the rich he has sent away empty.
He has come to the help of his servant Israel
for he has remembered his promise of mercy,
the promise he made to our fathers,
to Abraham and his children forever (Lk 1:46–55).
Glory to the Father and to the Son and to the Holy Spirit,
as it was in the beginning, is now, and will be forever.
Amen.

It is in the house of Elizabeth and Zechariah that Mary sings her song of praise. Perhaps these were the words that moved Zechariah from doubt to trust. Mary's motherhood is so extensive, conceiving the New Adam and, thus, in one way, conceiving all of us as well.

This mystical motherhood was not lost on the Church Fathers. Most often, they encourage us to imitate Mary and bring Christ forth in our hearts into the world as she did. That is, whereas Mary births Christ naturally, we are to do it supernaturally. "No one has dared to give so pure a revelation of the divinity of the Lord as John. We must make bold to say the Gospels are the fulfilment of the whole Bible and John's Gospel is the fulfilment of the Gospels. No one can grasp their meaning unless he has rested on Christ's breast, unless he has received Mary from Jesus so that she has become his mother too."[67] "What came about in bodily form in Mary, the fullness of the godhead shining through Christ in the Blessed Virgin,

---

[67] Origen, *Commentary on the Gospel of John*, 1.6. Clément, *The Roots of Christian Mysticism*, 98.

takes place in a similar way in every soul that has been made pure. The Lord does not come in bodily form, for "we no longer know Christ according to the flesh," but he dwells in us spiritually and the Father takes up his abode with him, the Gospel tells us. In this way the child Jesus is born in each one of us."[68]

My Lord Jesus, when You first entered Your own creation, You chose to remain hidden in our Mother's womb, as we all must. Show me the way to love You in the everyday, in the human, in the things I tend to ignore as too mundane or insignificant. As Advent begins to turn to Christmas, give me the grace to see how Your becoming flesh has changed everything about me and about this world where I live and love, pray, and will one day perish.

Come, Lord Jesus,
Come, Lord Jesus,
Come, Lord Jesus!
Amen.

Do I tend to think of Jesus more as God and not enough as a man? Do I appreciate how He was just like me in all things but sin? Think of that: everything I do that is without sin, Jesus Christ did as well—learn, make friends, laugh, enjoy beautiful sights and sounds, had a favorite food and place, etc.

Do I appreciate that sinning does not really belong to being human, then? To be human is to be totally one with God. In what parts of my humanity do I still keep God at a distance?

[68] Gregory of Nyssa (d. 395), *On Virginity* (PG 46,3 24 & 8 3 8); Clément, *The Roots of Christian Mysticism*, 251.

The flesh of Jesus Christ is holy flesh, God's own body. Two important implications arise from this. First, it sounds funny to say, but Christianity is a very materialistic religion in that, taking on human matter, the Son of God redeems the world through this incarnation and all that He does in and with that body. Perhaps God could have arranged it otherwise, but it was by the sending of His Son into the human condition which redeems the universe. This is why Catholics, especially, take the created order very seriously—why we teach philosophy and not just Scripture, for example, why we immerse ourselves into the political and economic spheres and don't distance ourselves too far from the world, why we have celebrations of feasting and an insistence on enjoying life deeply (e.g., Gaudete Sunday, the Christmas Octave, and all the Sundays, feast days, and holy seasons that mark our Catholic calendar).

Another implication of God's coming to earth is that Christianity cannot be understood simply as an otherworldly religion. Christ came not only to bring sinners into His own heavenly life but also to give us the grace to live this life, in this world, as virtuously and as wisely and as joyfully as possible. In other words, Christianity is not just about getting into heaven; it is also working here and now to love neighbor by cooperating with God's grace and God's ways in forming a more just society and more beautiful culture. That is why Christians must be on the front line of defending innocent human life, of proclaiming the integrity of the human person as body and soul, in understanding the role of the family and the meaning of sexuality and gender as God intends and not as fads seek to dictate. You must also continue the corporal and spiritual works of mercy in your everyday life:

> The corporal works of mercy, relieving bodily suffering: (1) to feed the hungry; (2) to give drink to the thirsty; (3) to clothe the naked; (4) to shelter the homeless; (5) to visit the sick; (6) to visit the imprisoned; (7) to bury the dead.
>
> The spiritual works of mercy, relieving spiritual torments: (1)

to instruct the ignorant; (2) to counsel the doubtful; (3) to admonish the sinners; (4) to bear patiently those who wrong us; (5) to forgive offenses; (6) to comfort the afflicted; (7) to pray for the living and the dead.

Among the most beautiful aspects of the Christian Faith is the intersection of humanity and divinity—that is, we treat God basically how we treat one another, and how we treat one another is usually how we treat God. In Jesus Christ, God and neighbor have become one, and we must pray to have the eyes and heart to live that way as of this very moment. That is why St. John the Evangelist writes:

> And yet I do write a new commandment to you, which holds true in him and among you, for the darkness is passing away, and the true light is already shining. Whoever says he is in the light, yet hates his brother, is still in the darkness. Whoever loves his brother remains in the light, and there is nothing in him to cause a fall. Whoever hates his brother is in darkness; he walks in darkness and does not know where he is going because the darkness has blinded his eyes. (1 Jn 2:8–11)

This selection is first an acknowledgement of the new law that Christ brings into the world—that each and every human person is worthy of our love. A Christian does not have the option to hate another or to ignore another as insignificant. To love God is to love the humans He puts into our lives. To say one loves God while still refusing to love his neighbor, John warns, makes one a liar, and he has obviously remade God into a distant image of his own image and likeness.

John's words here also recognize the inviolable dignity of our free will. God refuses to drag us into the light if we prefer the darkness. He will draw near only to those who allow Him. Think of the timeless prayer of the Our Father. There we daily ask God to forgive us our trespasses "*as we forgive* those who have trespassed against us." Here is a hint of how much like God we can be: we, too, can forgive others of their transgressions, but only if we allow God to forgive us. This is because any true forgiveness has only one font, the Lord, and any true forgiveness is not merely human in essence but is the effect of divine grace.

As the fourth week of Advent draws to a close, focus your attention on the Eucharist, the Most Holy Body and Blood of our Lord Jesus Christ. Is this not what Christmas is all about—the Son of God now embodied and visible? Here is the One whom all the prophets longed to see, the fulfillment of all your true desires as well. The Church is the creche continued; the Eucharistic meal extends the manger (from *mangiare*, "to eat"; think of the Italian command to eat, *mangia*!) to all the faithful across time and space.

This is why the city name of Bethlehem in Hebrew literally means "the house of bread." Once again, the Lord works quietly and cleverly to get our attention—of all the places He could have been born, He chose a place whose name would be the very means by which He continued His presence on earth until the end of days. As you kneel before the Nativity scene this Christmas, dwell upon the beautiful gift of the Eucharist and how we can prepare to receive Jesus more fruitfully into our lives.

> He was a baby and a child, so that you may be a perfect human being. He was wrapped in swaddling clothes so that you may be freed from the snares of death. He was in the manger so you could come to the altar. He was on the earth so you could be in the stars. He had no other place in the inn, so you that you may have many mansions in the heavens. "He, being rich, became poor for your sakes, that through his poverty you might be rich" (2 Cor 8:9). Therefore, his poverty is our inheritance, and the Lord's weakness is our virtue. He chose to lack for himself, so that he may abound for all. The sobs of that appalling infancy cleanse me, those tears wash away my sins. Therefore, Lord Jesus, I owe more to your sufferings because I was redeemed than I do to works for which I was created.[69]

---

69 St. Ambrose, *Exposition on the Gospel of Luke* 2.41–42; trans. Oden, *Luke: Volume 3 in the Ancient Christian Commentary on Scripture*, 37–38 (slightly adjusted).

He condescended to become incarnate at that time, that after His birth He might be enrolled in Caesar's taxing, and in order to bring liberty to us might Himself become subject to slavery. It was well also that our Lord was born at Bethlehem, not only as a mark of the royal crown, but on account of the sacrament of the name. But down to the very end of time, the Lord ceases not to be conceived at Nazareth, to be born at Bethlehem, whenever any of His hearers taking of the flour of the word makes himself a house of eternal bread. Daily in the Virgin's womb, i.e. in the mind of believers, Christ is conceived by faith, born by baptism. It follows, and she brought forth her firstborn son. He is also only-begotten in the substance of His divinity, firstborn in the taking upon Himself humanity, firstborn in grace, only begotten in nature. He who clothes the whole world with its varied beauty, is wrapped up in common linen, that we might be able to receive the best robe; He by Whom all things are made, is folded both hands and feet, that our hands might be raised up for every good work, and our feet directed in the way of peace. He is confined in the narrow space of a rude manger, whose seat is the heavens, that He may give us ample room in the joys of His heavenly kingdom. He Who is the bread of Angels is laid down in a manger, that He might feast us, as it were the sacred animals, with the bread of His flesh. He who sits at His Father's right hand, finds no room in an inn, that He might prepare for us in His Father's house many mansions; He is born not in His Father's house, but in an inn and by the way side, because through the mystery of the incarnation He was made the way by which to bring us to our country, (where we shall enjoy the truth and the life.).[70]

The next time you present yourself to receive Holy Communion, imagine yourself approaching that Host as if you were approaching the manger in Bethlehem.

[70] The Venerable Bede, *Commentary on Luke*, at Lk 2:6, accessed at: https://catenabible.com/lk/2.

Do you understand that the Eucharist is not just an effect of Jesus's love or power? It is Jesus! In assimilating this truth more and more, what changes might you see in your life?

> It was recognized, in fact, that this glorious flesh possessed the property common to all human beings: like them it was maintained with the help of bread. But this body partook of the divine dignity because of the indwelling of the Word. We are therefore entitled to believe that the bread hallowed by the Word of God is transformed to become the body of the Word. . . . As the bread transformed into that body was thereby raised to divine power, a similar change happens to the bread of the Eucharist. In the former case the grace of the Word hallowed the body that drew its substance from bread, and in a sense was itself bread. Likewise in the Eucharist the bread is hallowed by the Word of God and prayer. . . . It is transformed at once into his body . . . as expressed in these words: "This is my body." . . . That is why, in the economy of grace, he gives himself as seed to all the faithful. His flesh composed of bread and wine is blended with their bodies to enable human beings, thanks to their union with his immortal body, to share in the condition of incorruptibility.[71]

Extended Prayer Period: The Eucharist is the bond of charity for those who understand that here is Jesus Christ, the Lamb slain for the salvation of the world, but it is also unfortunately a stumbling block for those who ignore it or reduce it to a mere symbol or meal. Take some time to be with Jesus as John portrays this pivotal scene in his sixth chapter. Let Jesus's words help you see the Eucharist as he tries to explain it to those whose fidelity seems to hinge on this very topic—those who accept His Body and Blood as true food and

---

71 Gregory of Nyssa, *Catechetical Oration* 37; trans. Clément, *The Roots of Christian Mysticism*, 110.

true drink remain and grow in union with Jesus; those who refuse to believe this teaching leave Him, and their whereabouts are unknown to this day.

> The next day, the crowd that remained across the sea saw that there had been only one boat there, and that Jesus had not gone along with his disciples in the boat, but only his disciples had left. Other boats came from Tiberias near the place where they had eaten the bread when the Lord gave thanks. When the crowd saw that neither Jesus nor his disciples were there, they themselves got into boats and came to Capernaum looking for Jesus. And when they found him across the sea they said to him, "Rabbi, when did you get here?" Jesus answered them and said, "Amen, amen, I say to you, you are looking for me not because you saw signs but because you ate the loaves and were filled. Do not work for food that perishes but for the food that endures for eternal life, which the Son of Man will give you. For on him the Father, God, has set his seal."
>
> So they said to him, "What can we do to accomplish the works of God?" Jesus answered and said to them, "This is the work of God, that you believe in the one he sent." So they said to him, "What sign can you do, that we may see and believe in you? What can you do? Our ancestors ate manna in the desert, as it is written: 'He gave them bread from heaven to eat.'"
>
> So Jesus said to them, "Amen, amen, I say to you, it was not Moses who gave the bread from heaven; my Father gives you the true bread from heaven. For the bread of God is that which comes down from heaven and gives life to the world." So they said to him, "Sir, give us this bread always." Jesus said to them, "I am the bread of life; whoever comes to me will never hunger, and whoever believes in me will never thirst. But I told you that although you have seen [me], you do not believe. Everything that the Father gives me will come to me, and I will not reject anyone who comes to me, because I came down from heaven not to do my own will but the will of the one who sent me. And this is the will of the one who sent me, that I should not lose anything of what he gave me, but that I should raise it [on] the last day. For this is the will of my Father, that

everyone who sees the Son and believes in him may have eternal life, and I shall raise him [on] the last day."

The Jews murmured about him because he said, "I am the bread that came down from heaven," and they said, "Is this not Jesus, the son of Joseph? Do we not know his father and mother? Then how can he say, 'I have come down from heaven'?" Jesus answered and said to them, "Stop murmuring among yourselves. No one can come to me unless the Father who sent me draw him, and I will raise him on the last day. It is written in the Prophets: 'They shall all be taught by God.' Everyone who listens to my Father and learns from him comes to me. Not that anyone has seen the Father except the one who is from God; he has seen the Father. Amen, amen, I say to you, whoever believes has eternal life. I am the bread of life. Your ancestors ate the manna in the desert, but they died; this is the bread that comes down from heaven so that one may eat it and not die. I am the living bread that came down from heaven; whoever eats this bread will live forever; and the bread that I will give is my flesh for the life of the world."

The Jews quarreled among themselves, saying, "How can this man give us [his] flesh to eat?" Jesus said to them, "Amen, amen, I say to you, unless you eat the flesh of the Son of Man and drink his blood, you do not have life within you. Whoever eats my flesh and drinks my blood has eternal life, and I will raise him on the last day. For my flesh is true food, and my blood is true drink. Whoever eats my flesh and drinks my blood remains in me and I in him. Just as the living Father sent me and I have life because of the Father, so also the one who feeds on me will have life because of me. This is the bread that came down from heaven. Unlike your ancestors who ate and still died, whoever eats this bread will live forever." (Jn 6:22–58)

Why do you think Jesus was so insistent on making sure we understood this connection between His Body and the bread we consume?

Why do you think so many Christians refuse to see John 6 as a very clear declaration of the Eucharist, so firmly rooted in the Bible?

How do you think Jesus felt when some of His followers, up to this point, choose to abandon Him? If He did mean this teaching symbolically, would He not be a terrible teacher to allow some disciples to take this teaching literally and thus leave over the scandal?

What resonates most strongly with you to read that you have Jesus's own "life within you"?

Pour forth, we beseech you, O Lord, our grace into our hearts, that we, to whom the Incarnation of Christ your Son was made known by the message of an Angel, may by his Passion and Cross be brought to the glory of his Resurrection. Who lives and reigns with you in the unity of the Holy Spirit, God for ever and ever. Amen.

Week 5

Christmastime

From First Vespers of Christmas until the Presentation

℣. After childbirth, O Virgin, thou didst remain inviolate.
℟. Intercede for us, O Mother of God.

Let us pray.

O God, Who by the fruitful virginity of blessed Mary, hast given to mankind the rewards of eternal salvation: grant, we beseech Thee, that we may experience her intercession for us, through whom we deserved to receive the Author of life, our Lord Jesus Christ, thy Son.
℟. Amen.

The Church celebrates four distinct Christmas Masses: one as an anticipatory vigil on the evening of December 24, the traditional Midnight Mass, one at Christmas dawn, and one for Christmas day. The Gospels for the first three are what one would expect: the infancy narratives from Matthew and Luke, but the Christmas Mass during the day proclaims John's prologue, where the entire world hears how the Word of God has now become flesh.

The Vigil Mass (Years A, B, or C): Mt 1:1–25
The Mass during the night (Years A, B, or C): Lk 2:1–14
The Mass at dawn (Years A, B, or C): Lk 2:15–20
The Mass during the day (Years A, B, or C): Jn 1:1–18

Moreover, Christmas is not simply a jam-packed day; it is an entire Octave, the Church asking us to extend our celebrations for eight entire days. The Nativity of the Lord is too grand to last only one day but continues up through January 1 and the Church's celebration of Mary, Mother of God, but then there is the solemnity of the Epiphany of Our Lord (traditionally on January 6, thus the "twelve days of Christmas") as well as the Lord's presentation in the Temple on February 2.

Given all of these significant celebrations, it is understandable that the time when Christmas officially ends has undergone modifications over the years. Before Vatican II, the season of Christmas lasted for forty days, from December 25 to February 2. Now, Christmas lasts for eight days, the Octave of Christmas (analogous to the Octave of Easter), up to the celebration of Mary, Mother of God (January 1). But we also have the so-called twelve days of Christmas, and liturgically there is precedent, in that Christmastide had lasted until the feast of Epiphany on January 6. However, today—according to our conference of Catholic bishops—Christmas for us in the United States lasts through the Baptism of the Lord, celebrated on the first Sunday after Epiphany (or, when Epiphany Sunday falls on January 7 or 8, the Lord's Baptism is celebrated immediately on the following Monday).

When you attend one of the four possible Christmas Masses, the first pronouncement you may hear is the ancient timeline known today as *The Nativity of our Lord Jesus Christ*. This medieval calendar is originally found in the 1584 edition of *Roman Martyrology*, a post-Tridentine text cataloging the martyrs and saints of the Roman Rite. Each line recalls a significant event within salvation history, whether Christian or not, providing a beautiful tapestry of worldly and heavenly happenings uniting the human race as a whole and orienting all eyes on the nativity of Jesus in Bethlehem.

Although the spirit of Vatican II suppressed this Christmas pronouncement, St. John Paul II resurrected it at Midnight Mass in 1980.

The nativity of our Lord Jesus Christ according to the Flesh:

> The Twenty-fifth Day of December, when ages beyond number had run their course from the creation of the world, when God in the beginning created heaven and earth, and formed man in his own likeness; when century upon century had passed since the Almighty set his bow in the clouds after the Great Flood, as a sign of covenant and peace; in the twenty-first century since Abraham, our father in faith, came out of Ur of the Chaldees; in the thirteenth century since the People of Israel were led by Moses in the Exodus from Egypt; around the thousandth year since David was anointed King; in the sixty-fifth week of the prophecy of Daniel; in the one hundred and ninety-fourth Olympiad; in the year seven hundred and fifty-two since the foundation of the City of Rome; in the forty-second year of the reign of Caesar Octavian Augustus, the whole world being at peace, Jesus Christ, eternal God and Son of the eternal Father, desiring to consecrate the world by his most loving presence, was conceived by the Holy Spirit, and when nine months had passed since his conception, was born of the Virgin Mary in Bethlehem of Judah, and was made man.[72]

Starting from the creation of the world up through the birth of Jesus Christ, this proclamation teaches two major lessons. The first is that the God of Jesus Christ is the God of all, not just of Israel and not just of Christians. All of human history points to His providence: He is the cause, the sustainer, and the end goal of all that is. That is why the Church does not shy away from the natural order but is entirely based on the fact that God Himself enters the human. So, here we announce not only the world's creation but also

---

72 From the *Roman Martyrology*, accessed at: https://www.usccb.org/prayer-and-worship/liturgical-year-and-calendar/christmas/christmas-proclamation.

significant events, from the Great Flood to the Olympics to Roman rulers.

There are two lessons worth praying over here. The first is that all of human history is God's domain, and His loving providence is not limited to only the biblical or "religious" happenings. Accordingly, God can therefore be found in all things. The two "cities," as Augustine so aptly described them—the City of God and the City of Man—will run together and alongside each other until the final judgment. Accordingly, those in "the world" can always benefit from the Christian way of life, and those firmly at home in the Church can always learn from the world and (should) see in the most vile of their enemies a faint face of Christ Himself. This should also caution us from canonizing or condemning anyone too early—while alive on this earth, all constantly choose, and humility demands we see in everyone a sinner called to be a saint.

In this way, Christmas has ushered in a new way of understanding history—no longer a random, unrelated sequence of ultimately meaningless events, nor can it be said to be controlled by some uncaring fatalism. Surrounded by pagans and a culture where superstition and a sense of doom permeated everything, the Church Fathers keenly wrote against the unavoidable inevitability of the natural world. For the early Christians, history became where and how God works out the redemption of all mankind. It is His good creation; it is where and how He Himself assumed humanity to Himself; and it is where the final redemption of all will one day occur. It is in this very concrete arena of flesh, fur, and family, of work, woes, and wars, of pleasures, peace, and praise that God and man either collaborate or contend with one another to determine the eternity of each of us.

The second lesson comes at the end with the announcement of Christ's conception and birth. This is *the* historical event, and there will not be anything as revolutionary until His final return. No war, no dictatorship, no natural disaster will mean to history what the little town of Bethlehem has. In that way, we live in the "last days" as the Church Fathers were wont to put it. Irenaeus, for example, exhorts his flock:

> This then is the order of the rule of our faith, and the foundation of the building, and the stability of our conversation: God, the Father, not made, not material, invisible; one God, the creator of all things: this is the first point of our faith.
>
> The second point is: The Word of God, Son of God, Christ Jesus our Lord, who was manifested to the prophets according to the form of their prophesying and according to the method of the dispensation of the Father: through whom all things were made; who also at the end of the times, to complete and gather up all things, was made man among men, visible and tangible, in order to abolish death and show forth life and produce a community of union between God and man.
>
> And the third point is: The Holy Spirit, through whom the prophets prophesied, and the fathers learned the things of God, and the righteous were led forth into the way of righteousness; and who in the end of the times was poured out in a new way upon mankind in all the earth, renewing man unto God.[73]

The Annunciation and the visible birth of Christ at Christmas has traditionally been the delineators of all time, at least for us in the West, who mark history into two spans: BC, Before Christ, and AD, *Anno Domini*—in the Year of our Lord. The more "woke" folk today have no choice but to rely on this demarcation but, shying from anything explicitly Christian, have masked this marker with BCE—Before the Common Era—and CE—in the Common Era. Is this not what many have done to Christmas as well? We enjoy the glitz and the gifts but shy away from the Child and the creed.

---

[73] Irenaeus of Lyons, *The Demonstration of the Apostolic Preaching* §5–6, pages 75–76 when accessed at https://www.documentacatholicaomnia.eu/03d/0130-0202,_Iraeneus,_Demonstration_Of_The_Apostolic_Preaching,_EN.pdf.

Do you take time each night to reflect on your day, to thank God for two or three moments of grace, and perhaps ask forgiveness for one instance of sinful thought or behavior? Each day is your own personal history, and you and the Lord have either worked together or apart—think back on that.

Do you truly desire to form your life into a heaven on earth? If not, do you find yourself waiting to make that conversion, that firm resolve for a better habit? Do you ever really face your mortality and contemplate that this could very well be your "last" day or night, thus shaping your eternity?

Do you write people off as "lost" or, conversely, ever congratulate yourself for being "saved"? Pray to understand the fragility of one's salvation; pray to be more compassionately understanding of the travails and past hurts of those we might consider damned.

After four weeks, tonight's Mass will once again resurrect the singing of the Gloria. In having suppressed the Gloria during Advent, the Church has asked us to long for these words and to grow excited that they return on Christmas Eve, found yet again in the original mouths which first glorified God with these words:

> Glory to God in the highest. And on earth peace to men of good will.
>
> We praise You. We bless You. We adore you. We glorify You.

We give You thanks for Your great glory. O Lord God, heavenly King, God the Father almighty.

O Lord Jesus Christ, the Only-begotten Son. O Lord God, Lamb of God, Son of Father: You who take away the sins of the world, have mercy on us. You Who take away the sins of the world, receive our prayer. You Who sit at the right hand of the Father, have mercy on us. For You alone are holy. You alone are the Lord. You alone, O Jesus Christ, are most high.

Together with the Holy Spirit in the glory of God the Father. Amen.

Historians of liturgy trace the Gloria back to the seventh century. Rooted in the words of the Gospel of Luke and the angelic host gathered above where Mary had given birth to Jesus, the Gloria is a doxology giving glory to God (*doxa*, "glory" in Greek) and continuing the angels' words in a Trinitarian structure: "And suddenly there was a multitude of the heavenly host with the angel, praising God and saying: "Glory to God in the highest and on earth peace to those on whom his favor rests" (Lk 2:13–14).

Like the Sanctus and so many other prayers in the ancient Faith, the Gloria is Trinitarian: giving God glory for His kingly power, Jesus for taking away our sins and hearing our prayers, and the Holy Spirit, who is the very glory between the Father and the Son. In this way, the Gloria is a simple expression of the most profound mysteries of the Faith—the Trinity as well as the Incarnation, giving God thanks for having achieved the one perfect sacrifice through His divine humanity on the cross. It is a most universal hymn of praise—including not just followers of Jesus but all "people of good will." Yet again, we see how Christianity is not reserved for a particular people or has ever been confined to a particular place but is the expression of how every human heart was created to be and the goal of every human life.

Pray over the words of the Gloria. Does anything here strike you as beautiful, meaningful?

How do you understand the connection here between Jesus's taking away your sins and receiving your prayer? Do not make the mistake that He answers only the prayers of the sinless (that would only be Mary's), but the more you strive to live in accord with Christ and Christ's ways, the richer and more profound your prayer life will become.

When you pray that Jesus is "alone holy . . . alone the Lord, alone most high," can you admit that you are not? Any holiness or any "height" of living is, therefore, ultimately a gift of the Lord Jesus for you to enjoy.

Collect for the Solemnity of Christmas, Vigil Mass[74]

O God, who gladden us year by year as we wait in hope for our redemption, grant that, just as we joyfully welcome your Only Begotten Son as our Redeemer, we may also merit to face him confidently when he comes again as our Judge. Who lives and reigns with you in the unity of the Holy Spirit, God, for ever and ever.

[74] The Collect is the opening prayer you hear at Mass. It is so-called because its aim is to "collect" all themes of the prayers and readings for that day or week and summarize them into one introductory prayer.

As seen, Christmas has four different liturgies—the first being earlier on Christmas Eve, the Vigil Mass. The Gospel for this first Mass at Christmas offers an alternate, shorter Gospel than the entire first chapter of St. Matthew. We already prayed over the implications of Jesus's genealogy back in week 3. Let us now ask the Holy Spirit to lead us through the last seven verses of that chapter, the alternate reading for tonight's first Mass:

> Now this is how the birth of Jesus Christ came about. When his mother Mary was betrothed to Joseph, but before they lived together, she was found with child through the Holy Spirit. Joseph her husband, since he was a righteous man, yet unwilling to expose her to shame, decided to divorce her quietly. Such was his intention when, behold, the angel of the Lord appeared to him in a dream and said, "Joseph, son of David, do not be afraid to take Mary your wife into your home. For it is through the Holy Spirit that this child has been conceived in her. She will bear a son and you are to name him Jesus, because he will save his people from their sins."
>
> All this took place to fulfill what the Lord had said through the prophet: "Behold, the virgin shall be with child and bear a son, and they shall name him Emmanuel," which means "God is with us." When Joseph awoke, he did as the angel of the Lord had commanded him and took his wife into his home. He had no relations with her until she bore a son, and he named him Jesus. (Mt 1:18–25)

The Church's first Christmas Gospel brings us right into the majesty as well as the messiness of relationships—the relationship between humanity and divinity, as well as the many relationships between humans, between husband and wife, between parents and children, and so on.

This initial situation of Jesus's birth should provide each of us with many images and memories, petitions and concerns for prayer. God Himself descends into the structure of a family, into the love of a man and a woman, and—daresay—into the confusion of one man wondering what this is all about and what has happened to the life plans he has been carrying about for quite some time.

Like the other Joseph in the Old Testament (cf. Gn 37), God chooses to meet St. Joseph in a dream, and this carpenter proves to be a man who trusts his experience to discern the voice of God in whatever happens to him. Being "righteous," a word which then had the sense of being an upright Jewish person, faithful to the law and committed to the practices of Judaism, Joseph would not simply dismiss a sin as great as adultery, and so, in this sense, Joseph would have been compelled to expose his betrothed to the religious leaders. But Joseph, being *truly* righteous, knew that love must always triumph over law. So, confirmed by his dream that God was now at work in a new and singular way, Joseph trusted the Lord alive in him and acted accordingly.

Has your conscience ever struggled to follow Church teaching? How do you reconcile the Church's teachings and precepts with your own sense of what is right?

Do you dream? Do you remember your dreams? What do you do with them? In other words, how do you let those nighttime stories affect your waking life? Are you convinced that is God's speaking to you, or are you free enough to submit them to a higher standard of truth? Notice how Joseph followed his dream only because it was in perfect accord with love of God and love of neighbor, used to protect innocent life and not simply to achieve what he himself wanted.

> Dreams appearing to the soul in the love of God are sure signs of a healthy soul. They do not skip lightly from one image to another. They do not alarm the senses. . . . They fill the soul with spiritual happiness. Even after awakening, the soul seeks with an ardent desire the joy of the dream. Diabolical apparitions behave in contrary fashion. They change rapidly . . . they speak loudly, utter great threats, overwhelm the soul with their cries. Then the spirit, if it has been purified, recognizes them and awakens the body. . . . It may happen that good dreams do not bring joy to the soul but cause it sadness and tears without pain. That is the case with those who are making great progress in humility.[75]

Here we are invited to grow in spiritual discernment, learning how the voice of the Good Spirit speaks to us and how the enemy of our human nature acts in a contrary manner. The Holy Spirit's voice is recognizable by consoling stillness. Unlike Satan, the Good Spirit invites, He does not push; He reassures and does not drain you of trust in God's love; the Holy Spirit convicts those areas of your life where you still sin; He does not condemn you. The Holy Spirit illumines, while the enemy confuses. Satan shouts and overwhelms, is rapidly changing course and flitting about trying to throw us into a state of despair, hopeless that we'll never get it right. On the other hand, the Holy Spirit often consoles and comforts through tears, but they are tears "without pain," in that they are either out of contrition or joy, and those are the two ends of the continuum on which the Holy Spirit is at work.

But how are we to understand a verse that has divided Christians for the past five hundred years: the line that Joseph had "no relations" with Mary "until she bore a son"? Does this mean Jesus was the first of many children, or is there a deeper meaning?

> The deepening of faith in the virginal motherhood led the Church to confess Mary's real and perpetual virginity even in the act of giving birth to the Son of God made man. In fact,

---

75 Diadochus of Photike, *Gnostic Chapters*, §37; Clément, *The Roots of Christian Mysticism*, 169.

> Christ's birth "did not diminish his mother's virginal integrity but sanctified it." And so the liturgy of the Church celebrates Mary as *Aeiparthenos*, the "Ever-virgin."
>
> The Church has always understood these passages as not referring to other children of the Virgin Mary. In fact James and Joseph, "brothers of Jesus," are the sons of another Mary, a disciple of Christ, whom St. Matthew significantly calls "the other Mary." They are close relations of Jesus, according to an Old Testament expression.[76]

The Church has always preserved Mary's virginity, not because she did not love Joseph, and not because sexual intercourse between spouses is at all negative or second-rate, but because Mary was already consecrated to God as His spouse and beloved bride. This was certainly a lesson Joseph had at some point in time to learn; by all accounts, it seems he does so with great magnanimity. That is why the Church Fathers (and really anyone before 1600 and some of the later Protestant Reformers) argue that the two possibly misunderstood terms in this Gospel must be read intelligently in the light of the whole of the Faith.

When Jewish writings highlight a "firstborn," this does not necessarily mean that there is a second or a third. It simply marks a very significant moment in the life of a mother, in the life of a new family—one new life has been born unto them. As any parent can attest, there is something unrepeatably special about that first pregnancy, that first labor, that firstborn. "He had no relations with her until" is not a watershed indicating that Mary and Joseph now began to have sexual relations but, instead, the "until" here is more of a marker in time.

> "He did not know her until she gave birth to her firstborn Son." Based on this passage, some perversely suppose that Mary had other children, maintaining that a son is not called "firstborn" unless he has siblings. To the contrary, the divine Scriptures are accustomed to call someone "firstborn," not because other siblings come after him, but because he is born first.[77]

---

76 CCC §499–500.

77 St. Jerome, *Commentary on the Gospel of Matthew* 1.1.25; trans. Luigi

When someone resolves "not to smoke until I get to heaven" does not mean that St. Peter will be handing out cigars at the pearly gates. St. Paul wrote to the Catholics in Corinth that Jesus Christ "must reign until he has put all his enemies under his feet" (1 Cor 15:25). Does this mean that Jesus ceases reigning once He defeats His foes? By no means. In 1 Tm 4:13, we read how St. Paul tells St. Timothy that, "Until I come, attend to the public reading of scripture, to preaching, to teaching." Will Timothy then enter early retirement once Paul arrives? By no means. The "until," as used often in the New Testament, simply means a significant event has occurred in the ongoing narrative but does not demand a change in condition, let alone a reversal.

> "And when he had taken her, he knew her not, till she had brought forth her first-born Son." He [Matthew] has here used the word till, not that you should suspect that afterwards he did know her, but to inform you that before the birth the Virgin was wholly untouched by man. But why then, it may be said, has he used the word, "till"? Because it is usual in Scripture often to do this, and to use this expression without reference to limited times. For so with respect to the ark likewise, it is said, "The raven returned not till the earth was dried up" (Gen 8:7). And yet it did not return even after that time.[78]

> But concerning what the Evangelist said, "And he did not know her till she had borne her firstborn son," not a few careless people insist on asking whether after the Lord's birth the holy mother Mary had relations with Joseph. But this is not admissible on the grounds of either faith or truth. Far be it indeed that after the sacrament of so great a mystery and after the birth of the sublime Lord, one should believe that the

---

Gambero, *Mary and the Fathers of the Church: The Blessed Virgin Mary in Patristic Thought* (San Francisco: Ignatius Press, 1999), 207.

78 St. John Chrysostom, *Homily 5.5 on Matthew*, Homily on Mt 1:22–23, New Advent translation: https://www.newadvent.org/fathers/200105.htm#:~:text=And%20when%20he%20had%20taken,was%20wholly%20untouched%20by%20man.

Virgin Mary was intimate with a man. Remember that Miriam the prophetess of the Old Testament (the sister of Moses and Aaron) remained a virgin unsullied by man, having beheld the light of heavenly signs after the plagues of Egypt and the parting of the Red Sea and the Lord's glory going in advance and seen in a pillar of fire and clouds. It is not plausible therefore that the Mary of the Gospel, a virgin bearing God, who beheld God's glory not in a cloud but was worthy of carrying him in her virginal womb, had relations with a man. Noah, who was made worthy to converse with God, declared that he would abstain from the conjugal need. Moses, after hearing God calling him from the bush, abstained from conjugal relations. Now are we to believe that Joseph, the man who always did what was right, had relations with holy Mary after the birth of the Lord?[79]

He then goes on to say, that the adverb, "until," denotes a fixed time when that should take place, which had not taken place before; so that here from the words, "He knew her not until she had brought forth her first-born Son," it is clear, he says, that after that he did know her. And in proof of this he heaps together many instances from Scripture. To all this we answer, that the word "until" is to be understood in two senses in Scripture. And concerning the expression, "knew her not," he has himself shown, that it must be referred to carnal knowledge, none doubting that it is often used of acquaintance, as in that, "The child Jesus tarried behind in Jerusalem, and his parents knew not of it." So here the Evangelist informs us, in that wherein there might have been room for error, that she was not known by her husband until the birth of her Son, that we might thence infer that much less was she known afterwards. Lastly, I would ask, Why then did Joseph abstain at all up to the day of birth? He will surely answer, Because of the Angel's words, "That which is born in her" He then who gave so much heed to a vision as not to dare to touch his wife, would he, after he had heard the shepherds, seen the Magi, and known so

79 Chromatius of Aquileia (d. c. 407), *Tractate on Matthew*, accessed at: https://catenabible.com/com/585b63219ac03ecd4b8e6d53.

many miracles, dare to approach the temple of God, the seat of the Holy Spirit, the Mother of his Lord? From the words, "her first-born Son," some most erroneously suspect that Mary had other sons, saying that first-born can only be said of one that has brethren. But this is the manner of Scripture, to call the first-born not only one who is followed by brethren, but the first-birth of the mother. For if he only was first-born who was followed by other brethren, then no first-birth could be due to the Priests, till such time as the second birth took place.[80]

Do you try to read and understand Sacred Scripture in light of the entire Catholic Faith? It was the bishops of the Church who very early collated and canonized the books of the Bible as we have them today. The Bible must therefore be read from the fullness of the Faith. What could you do to increase your biblical literacy?

Do you pray over the Mass readings before coming to Church? They are easy to find online (https://bible.usccb.org/daily-bible-reading), and that is one way to pray with the word of God in an intentional way. If you can attend daily Mass, you can then hear what you prayed over liturgically and possibly gain even deeper insights from the homily.

Do you understand the Church's reasoning behind her very countercultural teachings on human sexuality and the goods of marriage? The Church's teaching against the indignities of artificial birth control, in vitro fertilization, as well as on the

80 St Jerome, *Commentary on Matthew* 1:25, accessed at https://catenabible.com/com/5735de4fec4bd7c9723b94ed.

beautiful complementarity of two genders only, and her unrelenting opposition to the murder which is abortion are all teachings that the world simply hates, and we must be strong in our understanding and defense of these human fundamentals.

Collect for the Christmas Mass at Midnight

O God, who have made this most sacred night radiant with the splendor of the true light, grant, we pray, that we, who have known the mysteries of his light on earth, may also delight in his gladness in heaven. Who lives and reigns with you in unity of the Holy Spirit, God, for ever and ever.

One of the more beloved Christmas traditions is Midnight Mass. Very often these days, "midnight" is held to be 10 or 11 p.m., but there is something special about getting to and from Church and praying the Mass late at night or very early in the morning. In her travels to the Holy land in 381 or 382, Egeria already attests to a Midnight Mass for Christmas, and by the twelfth century, it had become fairly standard across Europe. The Gospel you will hear proclaimed tonight is from Luke:

> In those days a decree went out from Caesar Augustus that the whole world should be enrolled. This was the first enrollment, when Quirinius was governor of Syria. So all went to be enrolled, each to his own town. And Joseph too went up from Galilee from the town of Nazareth to Judea, to the city of David that is called Bethlehem, because he was of the house and family of David, to be enrolled with Mary, his betrothed, who was with child.
>
> While they were there, the time came for her to have her child, and she gave birth to her firstborn son. She wrapped him in swaddling clothes and laid him in a manger, because there was no room for them in the inn. Now there were shepherds

> in that region living in the fields and keeping the night watch over their flock. The angel of the Lord appeared to them and the glory of the Lord shone around them, and they were struck with great fear.
>
> The angel said to them, "Do not be afraid; for behold, I proclaim to you good news of great joy that will be for all the people. For today in the city of David a savior has been born for you who is Messiah and Lord. And this will be a sign for you: you will find an infant wrapped in swaddling clothes and lying in a manger." And suddenly there was a multitude of the heavenly host with the angel, praising God and saying: "Glory to God in the highest and on earth peace to those on whom his favor rests." (Lk 2:1–14)

Luke's story of Jesus's birth begins with a Roman ruler who demanded to know the number of those who owed him allegiance. Joseph and Mary obeyed this census, certainly upset and saddened that a foreign potentate could control the movements of faithful Jewish families like theirs, for this was not an easy trip for anyone on foot.

Again, the Judeo-Christian story is rooted in actual times and places, confirmable through historically verifiable people. But into this world break in the angels, yet again repeating those words to Mary—"Be not afraid!" Why not? Because the King of Peace has been born this day in the city of David. And if you didn't think this birth was different from so many others, from all others, notice to whom this child has been born—"for you."

As the New Adam, the Christ Child has been born into all of our flesh. Yes, He was born to Mary in the natural order, as any child is born from his mother, but in the supernatural order, this baby is ours to hold and care for as well. In the words of Pope Leo, the Son of God "conforms" His divine life by coming down to each of our human lives, and in this way, He raises our sinfulness up to His splendor. If He were not "true God," He could not do the raising; if He were not "true man," He could not perform the descending.

> Such, then, dearly beloved, was the Nativity that befit Christ, "the power of God and the wisdom of God." By it he both conforms to us through humanity and rises above us through divinity. Were he not indeed true God, he could apply no remedy. Were he not indeed true man, he could not show example. Exulting angels sing at the Lord's Birth, "Glory to God in the highest," and proclaim, "On earth, peace to people of good will." They indeed see the heavenly Jerusalem being constructed from all the nations of the world. How much should the lowliness of human beings rejoice over this indescribable work of divine pity when the sublimity of angels so delights in it? . . .
>
> Realize, O Christian, your dignity. Once made a "partaker in the divine nature," do not return to your former baseness by a life unworthy [of that dignity]. Remember whose head it is and whose body of which you constitute a "member." Recall how you had been wrested "from the power of darkness and brought into the light and the kingdom" of God. Through the Sacrament of Baptism you were made "a temple of the Holy Spirit." Do not drive away such a dweller by your wicked actions and subject yourself again to servitude under the devil, because your "price" is the very blood of Christ, because he "will judge" you "in truth" who has redeemed you in mercy, Christ our Lord. Amen.[81]

Unlike the births we read about in the paper and online, this birth in Bethlehem has affected each of us in a most personal and intimate way. The Christ Child is "born unto us." As is the case also with the Crucifixion and Resurrection, Jesus Christ does not die and rise simply for a generic human race but for you and for each of us; here, He is not simply born to a Virgin Mother and foster father but is born unto each and every one of us. Through His humanity, He has entered our human nature, and in so doing, His divinity has now made us a partaker of God's own life. This means you no longer need to fall into those old bad habits or to think like one whose

---

81 St. Pope Leo the Great, *Sermon* 21.2–3; trans. Jane Patricia Freeland, *St. Leo the Great, Sermons* (Washington: DC: Catholic University of America Press, 1996), 79.

only security is financial or emotional. You have been made a son or daughter of God because the Son of God has this night been born unto you.

As you gaze upon the creche and the birth of Jesus, what do you want to tell Him?

How would you feel kneeling in the front of Church before the creche and asking Mary if she would let you hold her baby?

Pray over the words of the Gloria now that the angels have introduced it into the night sky—what images or words most strongly speak to you?

Collect for the Christmas Mass at Dawn

Grant, we pray, almighty God, that, as we are bathed in the new radiance of your incarnate Word, the light of faith, which illumines our minds, may also shine through in our deeds. Through our Lord Jesus Christ, your Son, who lives and reigns with you in the unity of the Holy Spirit, God, for ever and ever.

This morning the Church is invited to gather and root their day of Christmas festivities—or lonelinesses—in the celebration of the Eucharist. With the rising of the sun comes the lengthening of days, an apt reminder from nature that the Light is now shining in this world. The heart of this morning's Gospel is the maternity of Mary, the one who knows how this newborn child has come into the world, the one whose cooperation allows God to enter His own creation, and the one who—rightly so—reflects on all of these things in her heart.

> When the angels went away from them to heaven, the shepherds said to one another, "Let us go, then, to Bethlehem to see this thing that has taken place, which the Lord has made known to us." So they went in haste and found Mary and Joseph, and the infant lying in the manger. When they saw this, they made known the message that had been told them about this child. All who heard it were amazed by what had been told them by the shepherds. And Mary kept all these things, reflecting on them in her heart. Then the shepherds returned, glorifying and praising God for all they had heard and seen, just as it had been told to them. (Lk 2:15–20)

There are two psychological states featured here: the amazement upon the Good News that God has been born and the reflecting of Mary's heart. Perhaps these are two realities that have been forgotten today, but the more awed we allow ourselves to be by the beauty of the everyday, the more we take time to ponder its depth and significance.

How do you slow down? Do you? Have you arranged your day to make time—to literally carve it out—for stillness and silent prayer? Have you arranged a place, a "prayer chair" or any other comfortable way of being quiet in your house or office?

When you rest for this prayer time, what do you do? Do you reflect on the life God is asking you to live? Could you ask Mary to help you to know how to do this?

When we actually make time to open our eyes and allow ourselves to be struck with awe by all that surrounds us, our hearts and minds inevitably deepen as well. Our days are so rushed and our gaze so focused that we so often fail to notice the beauty surrounding us, the small ways people experience and express joy. And in a much larger way, we fail to be awed by the fact that all of these things actually exist. Have you ever stopped to consider that you *are*, that before you are this or that in life, you actually exist? As the ancient philosophical question went: Why is there anything rather than nothing? Once we begin to appreciate the fact that our Creator God has brought all of this into being, we can then begin to layer on all the other amazing gifts and blessings, experiences and relationships in our lives. This is the sense of awe all had at Bethlehem; this is the kind of treasuring God's goodness in our hearts that Mother Mary exemplifies.

But it doesn't stop even there. Once we ponder and contemplate the glories of God's goodness, we cannot help but to evangelize. We must share the fruits of Christ living in each of us—for He lives in you, and you have an experience of Him that no other creature could. Is this why we call our Church leaders "shepherds"? They must show us what it means to imitate those first evangelists who left Bethlehem and proclaimed, in whatever way they could, the fact that God is now with us.

> I too will proclaim the greatness of this day: the immaterial becomes incarnate, the Word is made flesh, the invisible makes itself seen, the intangible can be touched, the timeless has a beginning, the Son of God becomes the Son of Man, Jesus Christ, always the same, yesterday, today and for ever. . . . This is the solemnity we are celebrating today: the arrival of God among us, so that we might go to God, or more precisely, return to him. So that stripping off the old humanity we might put on the new; and as in Adam we were dead, so in Christ we might be made alive, be born with him, rise again with him. . . . A miracle, not of creation, but rather of re-creation. . . . For this feast is my perfecting, my returning to my former state, to the original Adam. . . . Revere the nativity which releases

you from the chains of evil. Honor this tiny Bethlehem which restores Paradise to you. Venerate this crib; because of it you who were deprived of meaning (in Greek, *logos*) are fed by the divine Meaning, the divine Logos himself.[82]

What does it mean for you to share the Good News of Christ's presence among us?

Do you ever excuse yourself from sharing the Gospel because you feel awkward or insufficiently trained? What could you do to overcome such obstacles?

Do you ever sense that your salvation is also somehow related to the salvation of those in your life?

Realize that shepherds were not learned men, but they were open to the gift of evangelical courage to go back to the wise and worldly to tell others what they had experienced. You are no different and, in fact, are probably much more capable on the human level than any of these sheep herders. What excuse do you give yourself for not speaking about Jesus more, or at least being more evangelically forthright about your Christian faith?

---

82 Gregory of Nazianzus, *Oration* 38; Clément, *The Roots of Christian Mysticism*, 41.

Does your spirituality have a natural movement throughout the day—perhaps praying for clarity in the morning, for perseverance midday, and in gratitude come the evening? One way to root your day in prayer is the traditional Morning Offering. If this is new to you, perhaps this Christmas morning you could make your gift to Jesus the promise to pray this every morning for the rest of your life:

> O Jesus, through the Immaculate Heart of Mary, I offer You all my prayers, works, joys, and sufferings of this day, in union with the Holy Sacrifice of the Mass throughout the world, in reparation for my sins, for the intentions of all my associates, and in particular for the intentions of the Holy Father this month.

You can find the Holy Father's monthly intentions easily enough online, but what is really important here is the offering of yourself, of your day. In this way, you exercise your priesthood of the faithful—not the sacrifice of the Holy Mass, but, in offering all you have before you, you do in fact unite your life's story to the story begun in Bethlehem and continued through Christ's Church each and every day.

Collect for Christmas Mass During the Day

O God, who wonderfully created the dignity of human nature and still more wonderfully restored it, grant, we pray, that we may share in the divinity of Christ, who humbled Himself to share in our humanity. Who lives and reigns with you in the unity of the Holy Spirit, God, for ever and ever.

One of the less-populated Masses is the Christmas Day Mass, so many people otherwise engaged in meals and merriment with family. Yet this quieter liturgy can be a very prayerful time for those who can plan accordingly. The Gospel for today proclaims the exquisite Prologue of John the Evangelist. Here, John recasts the creation story of Genesis in a more explicit Logocentric context—Logos meaning "the Word," which bestows an intelligibility and beauty to things. This Word is the Son of God, who has become flesh for us, empowering those willing to receive Him to also become a son or daughter of the same Father:

> In the beginning was the Word, and the Word was with God, and the Word was God. He was in the beginning with God. All things came to be through him, and without him nothing came to be. What came to be through him was life, and this life was the light of the human race; the light shines in the darkness, and the darkness has not overcome it.
>
> A man named John was sent from God. He came for testimony, to testify to the light, so that all might believe through him. He was not the light, but came to testify to the light. The true light, which enlightens everyone, was coming into the world. He was in the world, and the world came to be through him, but the world did not know him. He came to what was his own, but his own people did not accept him. But to those who did accept him he gave power to become children of God, to those who believe in his name, who were born not by natural generation nor by human choice nor by a man's decision but of God.
>
> And the Word became flesh and made his dwelling among us, and we saw his glory, the glory as of the Father's only Son, full of grace and truth. John testified to him and cried out, saying, "This was he of whom I said, 'The one who is coming after me ranks ahead of me because he existed before me.'" From his fullness we have all received, grace in place of grace, because while the law was given through Moses, grace and truth came through Jesus Christ. No one has ever seen God. The only Son, God, who is at the Father's side, has revealed him. (Jn 1:1–18)

Before Vatican II, this Prologue to St. John's Gospel was proclaimed at the end of every Latin Mass. So, why is this now the Church's last liturgical Gospel for Christmas Day? It was selected very early on as a summary of the most fundamental truths of the Faith—the Trinity ("the Word was with God, and the Word was

God "), the goodness of creation ("All things came to be through him, and without him nothing came to be"), the Incarnation ("And the Word became flesh"), His rejection by the perfidious ("He came to what was his own, but his own people did not accept him"), the saving adoption for those who do accept Him ("But to those who did accept him he gave power to become children of God"), and the early beginnings of the Christian Church and the salvation history into which we ourselves have been caught up as well ("A man named John was sent from God. He came for testimony, to testify to the light, so that all might believe through him. He was not the light, but came to testify to the light. The true light, which enlightens everyone, was coming into the world.").

Jesus, the Word which John the voice had announced weeks ago, is now visible. Emmanuel has made good on His promise—God is with us—present to us no longer from afar or in some "spiritual" way, but in the flesh and blood of our very own humanity. This is now the meaning of everything human. "The Word was made flesh . . . to destroy death and give life,"[83] not simply biological life, but the true life which means communion with God. Life for us is not a mere extension of days, but a deepening of personhood and our becoming fully alive.

St. John's inspiration to refer to the Second Person of the divine Trinity as the Word is significant. According to Augustine, "This Word is Being itself,"[84] which means that all beings are somehow related to the Word. This is the glorious tapestry that is the Father's creation, the world from which our own bodies are made and the world in which we spend every single moment of this life. That is why all things are now able to speak to us of God, as any piece of art or music can tell you something about the artist responsible for it.

Notice how the Prologue teaches that there is nothing that exists apart from the Word. Now all creatures belong to God, and

---

83 Irenaeus of Lyons, *Demonstration of the Apostolic Preaching,* §37; Clément, *The Roots of Christian Mysticism*, 89.

84 St. Augustine, *Homily* 2.2 on Jn 1:6–14; trans. Edmund Hill, *Homilies on the Gospel of John 1–40* (New York: New City Press, 2009), 55.

even the most insignificant plant or animal or even some meteorological condition can speak to us of God's power and providence:

> You heavens, bless the Lord, praise and exalt him above all forever. All you waters above the heavens, bless the Lord, praise and exalt him above all forever. All you powers, bless the Lord; praise and exalt him above all forever. Sun and moon, bless the Lord; praise and exalt him above all forever. Stars of heaven, bless the Lord; praise and exalt him above all forever. Every shower and dew, bless the Lord; praise and exalt him above all forever. All you winds, bless the Lord; praise and exalt him above all forever.
>
> Fire and heat, bless the Lord; praise and exalt him above all forever. Cold and chill, bless the Lord; praise and exalt him above all forever. Dew and rain, bless the Lord; praise and exalt him above all forever. Frost and chill, bless the Lord; praise and exalt him above all forever. Hoarfrost and snow, bless the Lord; praise and exalt him above all forever.
>
> Nights and days, bless the Lord; praise and exalt him above all forever. Light and darkness, bless the Lord; praise and exalt him above all forever. Lightnings and clouds, bless the Lord; praise and exalt him above all forever. Let the earth bless the Lord, praise and exalt him above all forever. Mountains and hills, bless the Lord; praise and exalt him above all forever.
>
> Everything growing on earth, bless the Lord; praise and exalt him above all forever. You springs, bless the Lord; praise and exalt him above all forever. Seas and rivers, bless the Lord; praise and exalt him above all forever. You sea monsters and all water creatures, bless the Lord; praise and exalt him above all forever. All you birds of the air, bless the Lord; praise and exalt him above all forever. All you beasts, wild and tame, bless the Lord; praise and exalt him above all forever.
>
> All you mortals, bless the Lord; praise and exalt him above all forever. O Israel, bless the Lord; praise and exalt him above all forever. Priests of the Lord, bless the Lord; praise and exalt him above all forever. Servants of the Lord, bless the Lord; praise and exalt him above all forever. Spirits and souls of the just, bless the Lord; praise and exalt him above all forever.

> Holy and humble of heart, bless the Lord; praise and exalt him above all forever. (Dn 3:59–87)

While natural creatures praise God simply by being what they are, those persons endowed with the untouchable gift of free will—angels and humans—must choose to praise God. While our very being bespeaks His creative hand, our intellects and wills must freely receive Him as Lord and Savior. All may gaze upon the creche, but not all kneel. All may hear Christmas this day, but not all will pay heed to what the truth behind the celebration is.

Does anything significant come to mind when thinking of Jesus as "the Word" of the Father? What words do you use to reveal your truest self? What words do you wish you did not use?

Do you value truth over efficiency, or might you sometimes sacrifice the fullness of the truth in order to get your way or to get something done?

Does your spiritual life have room for the world of nature? Do you take time to thank God for the material world in all its varied splendors? Does your spiritual life have room for your own sense of bodily health and well-being?

Since we are much more than merely natural creatures, the Creator will never force us to do anything against our will. We all belong to Him, but not all have freely accepted Him. That is why the battle against sin is less a fight between two opposite camps but more of a civil war. God has no equal enemy, and there are not two independent nations locked in conflict—we are all sons and daughters, and while some have seceded from the rightful bounty that could have remained theirs, our main goal in this fight is not to destroy them but to win them back and have them come home. The Father combats the sabotage against Him by sending His Son into this fracas to vivify and deify those who have remained faithfully by His side and to try to win back the rebels who can still be saved.

Because this is the case, the Church does not allow us to stay complacent in our new Christmas robes and slippers for too long. This Christ Child has been born not only to live but to die as well—He has come to call like-minded prayer warriors alongside Him in the battle to win back souls and to cultivate a world where the widow and the orphan have a home. It is especially to these the Son of God identifies Himself—the rejected, the forgotten, the lowly.

That is, the commander in chief has just arrived behind enemy lines and now identifies His own self with every man and woman, but especially the outcast. Some of God's children have taken arms up against Him, some have not, and each of us lives in a constant state of choosing sides. Why else would the next three days after Christmas joy celebrate and hold up for us the lives of martyrs? When the reforms of the Council of Trent (1545–63) finally solidified the liturgical calendar in 1570, the council fathers purposefully put these days of rather cruel and bloody imagery immediately following Christmas.

If we look at these three celebrations of December 26, 27, and 28, we see that the Church lauds those who laid their life down for the incarnate Christ. The Church also uses these lives to teach us the three ways of being a martyr. St. Stephen is the first and most obvious—one who was martyred freely in his action as well as in his desire to give all for Jesus. On the twenty-seventh, we celebrate the one apostle for whom we do not commemorate in red but in the sanctity of white, St. John the Evangelist. St. John was exiled to the island of Patmos and there, according to the oldest of traditions, would be the only of the faithful apostles who would die from natural causes. John the Beloved Disciple is thus a martyr in his desire to give all, but not in his actions, in that he was not directly executed by enemies of the Faith. Finally, the little ones whom Herod orders slaughtered clearly die for Jesus, but in their actions and not necessarily in their desires, being too innocent to understand what exactly was happening.

Collect for the Feast of St. Stephen, Martyr (December 26)

Grant, Lord, we pray, that we may imitate what we worship, and so learn to love even our enemies, for we celebrate the heavenly birthday of a man who knew how to pray even for his persecutors. Through our Lord Jesus Christ, your Son, who lives and reigns with you in the unity of the Holy Spirit, God, for ever and ever.

As recalled in Acts 7, St. Stephen (d.c. 36) was proven to be a martyr in both action and desire. "As they were stoning Stephen, he called out, 'Lord Jesus, receive my spirit.' Then he fell to his knees and cried out in a loud voice, 'Lord, do not hold this sin against them'; and when he said this, he fell asleep" (Acts 7:59–60). Here, the first Christian martyr imitates his loving Master not only in laying his life down but forgiving his persecutors in the very act costing him his life.

> For although Saint Stephen was ordained deacon by the apostles, he preceded the apostles themselves by a blessedly triumphant death. Thus one who was lesser in rank became the first in suffering, and he who was a disciple in rank came to be the teacher through martyrdom. . . . Stephen the martyr was the first voluntarily to requite the Lord for what he, together with the whole human race, received from the Lord. For death, which our Savior first deigned to suffer for all men, was first repaid to our Savior by Stephen. . . . With God's help let us prepare our hearts as far as we can for patience. Let us strive to act like doctors toward all wicked men, and let us hate their evil deeds but not the men themselves. Let us pray for all good

men that they may quickly have recourse to amendment of life. If we pray for this, he deigns to grant it to us.[85]

Is there anyone who you are finding more than difficult to forgive? What are the hurts and possibly even grudges in your psyche still? Could you ask St. Stephen to help you attain Jesus's grace to forgive those people?

Do you fear your death? Do you fear the death of your beloved? What do you fear most?

Are you comfortable praying with the "deceased," those Christian friends and family now in heaven? Remember, praying is a lot like singing—we can do it alone, but it is usually better in a choir!

Feast of St. John, Apostle and Evangelist (December 27)

O God, who through the blessed Apostle John have unlocked for us the secrets of your Word, grant, we pray, that we may grasp with proper understanding what he has so marvelously brought to our ears. Through our Lord Jesus Christ, your Son, who lives and reigns with you in the unity of the Holy Spirit, God, for ever and ever.

85 St. Caesarius of Arles (d. 543), *Sermon* 219 from *Sermons, vol. 3 (187–238)* in The Fathers of the Church Series, trans. Sr. Mary Magdelene Mueller (Catholic University of America Press, 1973), 128.

The one apostle for whom the Church does not celebrate with red vestments and cloths is John the Beloved, John the Evangelist. Having outlived the other eleven, John was sentenced to a life of exile on the Island of Patmos by the Roman emperor Domitian around the year 95. Tradition thus places St. John's death around 100, celebrated as a martyr in desire but not in action.

Having received unmatched graces, he is known in the Eastern Church as John the Theologian for his theologically packed writings. Along with his brother, James, and our first pope, Peter, John must have enjoyed a special intimacy with Jesus. He was not only known as "the Beloved" but comfortable enough with Jesus to lean on Him at a meal (see Jn 13:23). John was also chosen to be with Jesus in four pivotal moments—the Transfiguration (see Mt 17:1–8; Mk 9:2–8; Lk 9:28–36; 2 Pt 1:16–18), the healing of Jairus's daughter (see Mt 9:18–26; Mk 5:21–43; Lk 8:40–56), Jesus's time of agony in the garden of Gethsemane on Holy Thursday (see Mt 26:37), and, of course, under the cross with Mary as the Beloved Disciple was instructed to take her into his home (see Jn 19:26–27).

Legend tells us that John took Mary to his home in Ephesus (and that is why the Third Ecumenical Council, determining Mary's divine motherhood, was held in 431 in Ephesus, a place of great Marian devotion) and tended to her until she was assumed body and soul into heaven. The two left the Holy Land to go into modern-day Turkey around 44, after Herod had imprisoned Peter and had John's brother, James, put to death. "About that time King Herod laid hands upon some members of the church to harm them. He had James, the brother of John, killed by the sword, and when he saw that this was pleasing to the Jews he proceeded to arrest Peter also" (Acts 12:1–2).

While in exile on Patmos, a common place for Roman rulers to banish those deemed to be hostile to the state (which, for Romans, meant hostile to the gods and goddesses as well), the Holy Spirit inspired John to compose the book of Revelation as well, the final book of the Bible full of symbols and meaning. There, he tells the Church that he is sharing in the distress of all the persecuted, shoved through death's door for his fidelity to the Christ: "I, John, your brother, who share with you the distress, the kingdom, and the endurance we have in Jesus, found myself on the island called Patmos because I proclaimed God's word and gave testimony to Jesus" (Rv 1:9).

Have you been persecuted for the Faith? Like John, short of being put to the sword, have you experienced any worldly setbacks or sufferings because you remained faithful to the Gospel?

How are you feeling weaving all this talk of persecution and martyrdom with the joys of Christmas? Are you able to hold them together, or does it all seem contradictory? How do you reconcile these two aspects of the Faith?

Collect for the Feast of the Holy Innocents (December 28)

O God, whom the Holy Innocents confessed and proclaimed on this day, not by speaking but by dying, grant, we pray, that the faith in your which we confess with our lips, may also speak through our manner of life. Through our Lord Jesus Christ, your Son, who lives and reigns with you in the unity of the Holy Spirit, God, for ever and ever.

December 28 marks the macabre feast of the Holy Innocents (d. c. 0), martyrs in action but not in desire, having no way to will such a bloody end to their little lives. Yet God has rewarded their sacrifice by remembering them this day and in the eternal memory of his Church.

> When they had departed, behold, the angel of the Lord appeared to Joseph in a dream and said, "Rise, take the child and

> his mother, flee to Egypt, and stay there until I tell you. Herod is going to search for the child to destroy him." Joseph rose and took the child and his mother by night and departed for Egypt. He stayed there until the death of Herod, that what the Lord had said through the prophet might be fulfilled, "Out of Egypt I called my son." When Herod realized that he had been deceived by the magi, he became furious. He ordered the massacre of all the boys in Bethlehem and its vicinity two years old and under, in accordance with the time he had ascertained from the magi. Then was fulfilled what had been said through Jeremiah the prophet:
>
> "A voice was heard in Ramah, sobbing and loud lamentation;
> Rachel weeping for her children, and she would not be consoled,
> since they were no more." (Mt 2:13–18)

Quoting Jeremiah 31:15 here, Matthew records the slaughter of the Holy Innocents, a jarring celebration during the Christmas Octave, but a constant reminder of the fragility of life in this fallen world, especially in the hands of feckless leaders.

> Herod, wanting to destroy the Savior of the world . . . commanded that all children two years of age and under be killed, figuring the age according to the time that he had learned from the Magi. He thought that his edict would reach even to the Lord himself, the author of life. . . . Thus not without cause did the Lord testify about himself through Solomon and say the following: *Evil men will seek and not find me. For they hated wisdom and did not adopt the Word of the Lord, and they did not want it* (Prv 1:28–30).
>
> Well, then, all the babies were slain in Bethlehem. When these innocents died on Christ's behalf, they became the first martyrs on Christ's behalf, they became the first martyrs of Christ. And David is shown to give an indication of them, when he says, From the mouths of infants and nursing babies you have perfected praise because of your enemies, that you might bring ruin to the enemy and the avenger (Ps 8:3). For in this persecution even tiny infants and nursing babies are killed on Christ's behalf and attain to the martyrdom of perfected praise. The wicked King Herod is destroyed, he who

> had usurped the realm to avenge himself against the King of Heaven. Thus it is that those infants not unfittingly have stood forth as blessed in all ways, who deserved to be the first to die for Christ, our Lord and Savior, to whom is the praise and glory in the ages of ages. Amen.[86]

While patristic sermons abound for this sad scriptural scene, Christmas carols have also depicted the sorrow of the moment. The Coventry Carol, for example, dates back to mid-sixteenth-century England, originally part of a mystery play uncovering the many nuances and depths of Christmas. The lyrics imagine the mothers of the innocents singing a final lullaby to their little ones, and in so doing, trying to comfort one another:

> Lully, lullay, thou little tiny child,
> Bye bye, lully, lullay.
> Thou little tiny child,
> Bye bye, lully, lullay.
>
> O sisters too, how may we do
> For to preserve this day
> This poor youngling for whom we sing,
> "Bye bye, lully, lullay?"
>
> Herod the king, in his raging,
> Chargèd he hath this day
> His men of might in his own sight
> All young children to slay.
>
> That woe is me, poor child, for thee
> And ever mourn and may
> For thy parting neither say nor sing,
> "Bye bye, lully, lullay."

---

86 St. Chromatius of Aquileia (d. 407), *Sermons and Tractates on Matthew*, trans. Thomas Scheck (Mahwah, NJ: Paulist Press, 2018), 119.

A much more recent carol (dating back to the early twentieth century) is the Holly and the Ivy. Here, the smooth brilliance of ivy is woven together with the harsh and spiny edges of the holly leaves. Once again, we are confronted with the Lord's descent into this "vale of tears," a call to arms of love and mercy. Here, too, we are brought into the world of nature, which speaks to us of God's creative power and the ability of all things to speak to us of the permeance of the Word:

The holly and the ivy,
When they are both full grown,
Of all the trees that are in the wood,
The holly bears the crown.
The rising of the sun
And the running of the deer,
The playing of the merry organ,
Sweet singing in the choir.

The holly bears a blossom,
As white as the lily flower,
And Mary bore sweet Jesus Christ,
To be our sweet Saviour.
The rising of the sun etc.

The holly bears a berry,
As red as any blood,
And Mary bore sweet Jesus Christ
For to do us sinners good.
The rising of the sun etc.

The holly bears a prickle,
As sharp as any thorn,
And Mary bore sweet Jesus Christ
On Christmas Day in the morn.
The rising of the sun etc.

The holly bears a bark,
As bitter as any gall,
And Mary bore sweet Jesus Christ
To redeem us all.
The rising of the sun etc.

The holly and the ivy,
When they are both full grown,
Of all the trees that are in the wood,
The holly bears the crown.
The rising of the sun etc.

Extended Prayer Period: Reflection on the Significance of Family.

Church's Liturgical Instruction: The feast of the Holy Family should be celebrated on the first Sunday after Christmas. When a Sunday does not occur between December 25 and January 1, it is to be celebrated on December 30.

Christianity is not a religion of rules but of relationships. It has more to do with family than with formulas. From the interpersonal relationships of the Trinity, to the incarnation of Christ lived out in the context of a mother and foster father, to the Church as an inextricably linked Body of adopted sons and daughters, the Christian Faith is all about consecrated connectedness.

Collect for the Feast of the Holy Family

O God, who were pleased to give us the shining example of the Holy Family, graciously grant that we may imitate them in practicing the virtues of family life and in the bonds of charity, and so, in the joy of your house, delight one day in eternal rewards. Through our Lord Jesus Christ, your Son, who lives and reigns with you in the unity of the Holy Spirit, God, for ever and ever.

> While he was still speaking to the crowds, his mother and his brothers appeared outside, wishing to speak with him. Someone told him, "Your mother and your brothers are standing outside, asking to speak with you." But he said in reply to the one who told him, "Who is my mother? Who are my brothers?" And stretching out his hand toward his disciples, he said, "Here are my mother and my brothers and sisters. For whoever does the will of my heavenly Father is my brother, and sister, and mother." (Mt 12:46–50)

To bring the Octave of Christmas to a close, pray over your experience of family and all that means. It was here you were conceived, however precarious your beginnings, you are alive today because someone cared more about you than for themselves. You have a mother and a father; you probably have a sibling or two or more, and you might even know extended families as grandparents, cousins, aunts, and uncles.

> What are the "virtues of family life" you best practice? Least practice?
>
> With which family member do you most struggle? Why, what is it about that person?
>
> Is "family" a primary image for your Christian life as well?

Take some time to pray over how much these people mean to you. If you are married, begin with your spouse and then pray over each of your children. Walk about your house and see all the photos of the many faces dear to you, and you to them. Bring to mind what you love about each of them and, concretely, how you have hopefully made their lives better.

Now think of belonging to Jesus's family. You are His adopted brother or sister, both children of God the Father and Mary your Mother. The saints are now your siblings, and as we have it from Jesus Himself from the Gospel above, all who hear God's voice and do His will are brother and sister and even mother to Him.

> Since the Virgin Mary's role in the mystery of Christ and the Spirit has been treated; it is fitting now to consider her place in the mystery of the Church. The Virgin Mary is acknowledged and honored as being truly the Mother of God and of the redeemer. She is clearly the mother of the members of Christ since she has by her charity joined in bringing about the birth of believers in the Church, who are members of its head. Mary, Mother of Christ, Mother of the Church.[87]

The great spiritual masters described intimacy with Christ in familial terms. For instance, think of the three reasons one might follow Jesus. The first is the slave mentality, the person who tries to do what is right simply to avoid correction or escape punishment. This person is usually filled with fear, and the magnificence of Christ's person is meaningless as long as I can be spared of hell. The second is the mentality of the soldier, the one who tries to do what is right solely because of the payoff at the conclusion of the fight. This kind of person is opportunistic and is faithful to Jesus for what Jesus can give back in return. The third kind of Christian is the one who owns how he or she is a son or daughter—the person who strives to follow Jesus simply for who Jesus is. This is a disinterested kind of love, inattentive to the rules and reasons, but more interested in being close to the Beloved.

Ironically, in many ways, it is "easier" to be a runaway or an orphan. Sadly, as one without guardians, there are no expectations or

---

[87] CCC §963.

demands put on you. There is no one asking where you are going or what you are doing, no one caring with whom you are spending time or what you are becoming. When we are immature, this may seem attractive, but Jesus reveals to us the great paradox of love—namely, to lay His life down for the sake of others—"Son though he was, he learned obedience from what he suffered" (Heb 5:8). It is "suffering" to live for others and to love them even when we do not naturally feel like it. It is not natural to receive another into your life as another self, but it is supernatural, and that is precisely what Christmas is all about, the Lord's desire to graft onto Himself a multitude of believers who will be for Him a Mystical Body throughout all space and time.

Where do you see yourself following Christ—slave, soldier, or son or daughter?

Do you ever pray a prayer of surrender to the Lord, allowing Him to have and to rely on you however He best sees fit?

Can you pray to love all those in your life, enemies included, as you love those closest to you?

Do you treat those whom you love as an extension of yourself, as those in whom your own joy and sorrows (and theirs, yours) are shared?

Today is born of a virgin he who holds the whole creation in his hand. He whose essence non can touch is bound in swaddling clothes as a mortal man. God, who in the beginning fashioned the heavens, lies in a manger; he who rained manna on his people in the wilderness is fed on milk from his mother's breast. The Bridegroom of the Church summons the wise men; the Son of the virgin accepts their gits . . . we worship thy birth, O Christ!

—Orthodox Christian Sticheron at the Ninth Royal Hour

Week 6

January 1 through Epiphany

In the first week of January, the Church moves from honoring Mary as the Mother of God (a title that did not come easily) to the solemnity of the Epiphany. Included during this time are also commemorations of the naming as well as the circumcision of Jesus.

A tradition arose in monasteries and religious houses that the first of the new year would be welcomed in by the ancient hymn the *Te Deum*. The words to this song of praise date back to the fourth century and possibly have St. Ambrose as their author. The hymn situates the content of the Apostles' Creed in a more celebratory tune, focusing in on all that God is and has done for those who resolutely place their hope in Him:

> You are God, we praise you:
> You are the Lord: we acclaim you;
> You are the eternal Father:
> All creation worships you.
> To you all angels, all the powers of heaven,
> Cherubim and Seraphim, sing in endless praise:
>   Holy, holy, holy, Lord God of power and might,
>   Heaven and earth are full of your glory.
> The glorious company of apostles praise you.
> The noble fellowship of prophets praise you.
> The white-robed army of martyrs praise you.

Throughout the world, the holy Church acclaims you:
 Father of majesty unbounded,
 Your true and only Son, worthy of all worship,
 And the Holy Spirit, advocate and guide.
You, Christ, are the King of Glory
The eternal Son of the Father.
When you became man to set us free,
You did not spurn the Virgin's womb.
You overcame the sting of death,
And opened the kingdom of heaven to all believers.
You are seated at God's right hand in glory.
We believe that you will come and be our judge.
Come then, Lord, and help your people,
Bought with the price of your own blood,
And bring us with your saints to glory everlasting.
Save your people, Lord, and bless your inheritance.
Govern and uphold them now and always
Day by day we bless you.
We praise your name forever.
Keep us today, Lord, from all sin.
Have mercy on us, Lord have Mercy
Lord, show us your Love and Mercy
for we put our trust in you.
In you, Lord, is our hope:
and we shall never hope in vain.

This new week of retreat begins with a New Year and, fittingly, with a pause before Mary, the Mother of God, to thank her for all she experienced bringing Jesus into this world. It is the eighth day after His birth, and with that, not only a new year but a new age has broken into human history. If we think about it, the events of the Annunciation and of Christmas actually began with Mary's Immaculate Conception, God's preparing a fitting mother for His only-begotten Son. Where the first stage of human history began with Adam, this last age has begun with the New Eve, the one whose entire life would be to "magnify the Lord" (Lk 1:46). So, if

God began with Mary, so should we begin our New Year thanking her for becoming the Mother of God.

Eight days after Christmas is also the feast of the Circumcision of the Christ Child: "When eight days were completed for his circumcision, he was named Jesus, the name given him by the angel before he was conceived in the womb" (Lk 2:21). An early sign of God's covenant with His people (see Gn 17:12), male circumcision became a central part of the Mosaic Law as an external sign of God's unwavering fidelity. A woman was to bring her son to the temple on the eighth day and then remain in seclusion for another thirty-three days (thus providing biblical precedent for celebrating some aspect of Christmas for forty days through the feast of Candlemas on February 2):

> The Lord said to Moses: "Tell the Israelites: When a woman has a child, giving birth to a boy, she shall be unclean for seven days, with the same uncleanness as during her menstrual period. On the eighth day, the flesh of the boy's foreskin shall be circumcised, and then she shall spend thirty-three days more in a state of blood purity; she shall not touch anything sacred nor enter the sanctuary till the days of her purification are fulfilled." (Lv 12:1–4)

In 1969, when the Church reorganized the liturgical year for the Roman Rite, the feast of the Circumcision was placed into a wider context, and January 1 became the solemnity of Mary, Mother of God, recalling both the circumcision as well as the naming of Jesus, but also adding a universal call to all people of good will, the World Day of Peace. In his 1974 Apostolic Exhortation *Marialis Cultus*, Pope Paul VI looked back at this change declared:

> In the revised ordering of the Christmas period, it seems to us that the attention of all should be directed towards the restored Solemnity of Mary the holy Mother of God. This celebration, placed on January 1 in conformity with the ancient indication of the liturgy of the City of Rome, is meant to commemorate the part played by Mary in this mystery of

salvation. It is meant also to exalt the singular dignity which this mystery brings to the "holy Mother . . . through whom we were found worthy to receive the Author of life."(17) It is likewise a fitting occasion for renewing adoration of the newborn Prince of Peace, for listening once more to the glad tidings of the angels (cf. Lk. 2:14), and for imploring from God, through the Queen of Peace, the supreme gift of peace. It is for this reason that, in the happy concurrence of the Octave of Christmas and the first day of the year, we have instituted the World Day of Peace, an occasion that is gaining increasing support and already bringing forth fruits of peace in the hearts of many.[88]

Solemnity of the Blessed Virgin Mary,
Mother of God (January 1)

O God, who through the fruitful virginity of Blessed Mary bestowed on the human race the grace of eternal salvation, grant, we pray, that we may experience the intercession of her, through whom we were found worthy to receive the author of life, our Lord Jesus Christ, your Son. Who lives and reigns with you in the unity of the Holy Spirit, God, for ever and ever.

The Gospel for today once again recalls how Mary's heart was immaculately large enough to hold all the mysteries of her Son's life. Amazement and joy are the feelings highlighted, and how could they not be? God has finally visited His people, not from afar, not from a mountain top, but from the birth of His Son—God now has a face and hands, God can now be held, God can finally be one of His own.

The shepherds went in haste to Bethlehem and found Mary and Joseph, and the infant lying in the manger. When they

88 Pope Paul VI, *Marialis Cultus* §5, https://www.vatican.va/content/paul-vi/en/apost_exhortations/documents/hf_p-vi_exh_19740202_marialis-cultus.html.

> saw this, they made known the message that had been told them about this child. All who heard it were amazed by what had been told them by the shepherds. And Mary kept all these things, reflecting on them in her heart. Then the shepherds returned, glorifying and praising God for all they had heard and seen, just as it had been told to them. When eight days were completed for his circumcision, he was named Jesus, the name given him by the angel before he was conceived in the womb. (Lk 2:16–21)

On the eighth day of Christmas, the Church remembers two very Jewish practices—the naming and the circumcision of a male newborn—while honoring Mary as the Mother of God. In the minds of the Church Fathers, circumcision had become a metaphor for cutting away anything that was not necessary. The great biblical exegete, Origin of Alexandria, uses circumcision to examine how to read Scripture, paring away all that is not life-giving:

> The first aspect of Scripture, that of the letter, is bitter enough. It prescribes circumcision of the flesh, regulates sacrifices and all that is meant by the "letter that kills." Reject all that as the bitter rind of the almond. In the second stage you will reach the defenses of the shell, the moral teaching, the obligation of self-control. These things are needed to protect what is kept inside. But they have to be broken, and assuredly there will be found enclosed and hidden beneath these wrappings the mysteries of God's wisdom and knowledge that restore and nourish the souls of the saints. This threefold mystery is to be seen throughout all Scripture.[89]

Here we see how the Church Fathers never dismissed a Jewish practice but either reframed it or spiritualized it, knowing how God's first chosen people were given not yet the fullness of right religion but its roots and earliest beginnings. Because of that trajectory, the Fathers reinterpreted much of what the Jews said and did in

---

[89] Origen, *Homilies on Numbers*, §9.7; Clément, *The Roots of Christian Mysticism*, 99.

order to amplify how God was at work. What was no longer needed became a foreshadowing of what God ultimately desired—for example, the crossing of the Red Sea became a prefiguring of the true freedom of Baptism, or the blood sacrifice of animals, understood as an anticipation of the true sacrifice of Christ on the cross.

It was the same with the uniquely human phenomenon of naming another, first given to Adam in the Garden of Eden (see Gn 2:19). Also, God's second commandment is to keep His Holy Name sacred (see Ex 20:7; Dt 5:11) and not bandy it about like any other personal reference. This is why the naming of a Jewish boy was a rather significant (and even public) event in the life of God's people. Remember the consternation caused by Zechariah's unwillingness to give his and Elizabeth's boy a familial name but instead go with a name unused in their clan, John (see Lk 1:59–66). The biblical authors emphasized the power of the Holy Name of Jesus, proven to accomplish miraculous deeds:

> If we are being examined today about a good deed done to a cripple, namely, by what means he was saved, then all of you and all the people of Israel should know that it was in the name of Jesus Christ the Nazorean whom you crucified, whom God raised from the dead; in his name this man stands before you healed. He is "the stone rejected by you, the builders, which has become the cornerstone." (Acts 4:9–11, quoting here Ps 118:22)

> Rather, he emptied himself, taking the form of a slave, coming in human likeness; and found human in appearance, he humbled himself, becoming obedient to death, even death on a cross. Because of this, God greatly exalted him and bestowed on him the name that is above every name, that at the name of Jesus every knee should bend, of those in heaven and on earth and under the earth, and every tongue confess that Jesus Christ is Lord, to the glory of God the Father. (Phil 2:7–11)

When Jesus taught His disciples to pray, He gave the Church the "Our Father," where in we are told to hallow God's name. Here, the great Augustine wrote to a wealthy widow who was searching how to pray now that she had to flee the Sack of Rome in 410 that, "When, therefore, we say, *May your name be made holy* (Mt 6:9), we remind ourselves to desire that his name, which is always holy, may be also held holy among human beings, that is, that it may not be scorned. This is something that benefits human beings, not God."[90]

Pray over your own name; search out its etymology. What resonates with you when pondering the name you have been given?

Do you keep the names of God "hallowed," or do you have a hard time keeping the second commandment?

Pray over the names you have bestowed in your lifetime. Do you see what a godly gift this is: to be able to help another form his or her identity?

While the circumcision and the naming of Jesus are commemorated on the eighth day after His birth, these are subsumed under the solemnity celebrated on January 1, Mary, Mother of God. This title was contested in the early Church, with some questioning how a mortal woman could rightly be invoked as God's mother. Of course, Mary is the mother of the Son only as incarnate, and, of course, she cannot be imagined as the mother of the Father or of the Holy

---

90 St. Augustine, *Letter* 130.11.21 to Proba (dated c. 411); trans. Roland Teske, *Letters 100–155* (Hyde Park: New City Press, 2003), 193.

Spirit. This had to be hammered out during the Church's Third Ecumenical Council, the Council of Ephesus in 431.

Here, somewhere between 200 and 250 bishops (ancient attendance lists vary) gathered at the Church of St. Mary in Ephesus, where, as mentioned, John had supposedly taken Mary into his home as instructed by Jesus. The council opened by reaffirming the Nicene Creed, as we still profess on Sundays and major feasts, and then went on to lay out the contrasting opinions of Nestorius, who would call Mary *Christokos*, the bearer of Christ, and of Cyril of Alexandria, who insisted Mary be called *Theotókos*, the bearer of God.

Nestorius was concerned that if Mary was truly the mother of all that Jesus is and does, she would be elevated equal to or even above God Himself, and all in attendance knew that was total blasphemy. To avoid exalting Mary to such a degree, this very influential patriarch of Constantinople forbade his congregation and religious houses under his control from invoking Mary as "Mother of God." Because the majority of Christians held this title dear, a division in one of Christianity's most important cities arose, and the emperor, fearing any division, called a meeting of all the Church's bishops in Ephesus (modern-day Turkey) in the summer of 431.

As with any Marian doctrine, at stake here was first and foremost Mary's proper title (although that proved to be the initial spark), but what ultimately had to be resolved was how best to understand the coming together of Jesus's two natures. Whereas Nestorius was comfortable keeping Jesus's divinity only "next to" His humanity, imagining Him dwelling in two separable or even temporarily disposable natures—and thus conceiving of Mary only as the mother of Jesus's humanity—the Church's main protagonist, Cyril of Alexandria (d. 444), thought differently.

Nestorius held that the natures were bound by a moral agreement, imagining Jesus as sort of two beings living side by side under the same skin. At one time He is divine, at other times human. Cyril, however, insisted that the Lord's unity between divinity and humanity is personal, involving all of who Jesus is, and that is why the term "hypostatic" is officially used—a Greek word meaning "personal," with the sense of very intimate as, the very source of one's entire existence.

In this way, there is nothing that the divine Son of God does not do that is not human, and vice versa. Now we can truthfully say that when Jesus asks for bread, God is hungry; when Jesus weeps, we can literally say God sorrows. Conversely, in Christ we can now say mankind can love enemies, pray for persecutors, defeat death, and live with the Father forever. Jesus is not at one time human and another divine; He is now and forever the Godman, whose natures cannot be divided or separated (this is precisely what the next council, the Council of Chalcedon in 451, will formalize further).

While this may sound more like some abstract theological debate stuck in the dustbin of ancient history, the title of Mary is essential not so much for understanding who she is but for a clear picture of her Son, Jesus. If Mary could not be considered the mother of the entire Messiah, Jesus Christ, fully human and fully divine, He would have entered this world—would have become incarnate—in an unusual and inhuman way. If the womb in which the unborn is in is not the womb of his mother, what then is she? What then is he? The Church has always refused to reduce Mary to just a vessel through whom the Son of God comes; the Church has always refused to think the Son of God entered this world apart from the natural care of a mother. Accordingly, Mary is truly mother, who gives the Son of God human life and the one from whom He receives all that makes Him man.

Do you tend to think of Jesus as two realities—perhaps more "really God" and not truly human like yourself, or perhaps you tend to think of Him as one of the guys and perhaps downplay the truth that He is truly the eternal Son of God, the Second Divine Person of the Trinity?

Do you ever stop and think of how Mary might have felt in all of this? She is alone, unsure of exactly what is going to happen, yet she trusts and lives day by day in the confidence that her God the Father will not only protect her but make something wonderfully great out of her life. Where might you see yourself in this unfolding of true Christian trust?

At the Council of Ephesus, Cyril helped the Church lay down twelve anathemas—statements that must be believed at the risk of periling one's own soul. For your prayer, slowly study *anathemas* 3, 4, and 5 and see how your head and heart can work together. That is, the more accurately we know who Jesus Christ is, the more ardently we can love Him, a truth that goes for any personal relationship.

> *Anathema* 3: If anyone shall after the hypostatic union divide the hypostases in the one Christ, joining them by that connection alone, which happens according to worthiness, or even authority and power, and not rather by a coming together, which is made by natural union: let him be anathema.
>
> *Anathema* 4: If anyone shall divide between two persons those expressions which are contained in the Evangelical and Apostolical writings (i.e., divide Jesus into a human person alongside a divine person), or which have been said concerning Christ by the Saints, or by himself, and shall apply some to him as to a man separate from the Word of God, and shall apply others to the only Word of God the Father, on the ground that they are fit to be applied to God: let him be anathema.
>
> *Anathema* 5: If anyone shall dare to say that the Christ is a *Theophorus* [that is, God-bearing] man and not rather that he is very God, as an only Son through nature, because the Word was made flesh, and has a share in flesh and blood as we do: let him be anathema.[91]

91 Extracts from the *Acts of the Council of Ephesus*, accessed at: https://www.newadvent.org/fathers/3810.htm.

See how carefully the Church works to understand how one divine person, the Son of God, can now be wholly human as well? The union of these two natures is not something side-by-side that can be taken on and off, discarded like membership in a club or coming home after visiting some foreign country. Rather, Jesus's union of divinity and humanity might be more like the television show Undercover Boss.

In this once popular program, the CEO of some company becomes one of his own employees and suffers the indignities of a new hire, chooses to work as "one of the guys," and, in so doing, learns what it is like to be a just another hire. Of course, like any analogy, one can push this parallel only so far (because, unlike the incarnation, the boss here eventually returns to his or her desk), but the image partially works because this is what the Son of God works on our behalf come Christmas: He chooses to be nothing other than one of us and so "empties" (cf. Phil 2:7) Himself of all glory so as to be one with us inglorious folks.

He cannot simply zoom back into heaven, nor can He throw off His mortality when things get tough (and, again, this is where the analogy with Undercover Boss fails). He is not a divine avatar only acting human but is truly man and henceforth lives all His godliness through the humanity, physicality, and even limitations of what it means to be human.

> Do you see how, on account of this union between divinity and humanity, the word of the apostolic teaching makes a common confession of Christ? For Jesus was not mere man prior to the communion and union of God with him, but the same Logos, having come into the Blessed Virgin herself, took to himself his own temple from the essence of the Virgin. He went forth from her as a man and was seen to be a man externally, although interiorly he existed as true God. Therefore, after his birth, he preserved the virginity of his Mother, although this is not true of any of the saints. The saints were by nature human beings and so they all underwent an equally human birth. But, because he was God by nature, when in this last time he also took the human condition, he revealed

> the birth from the Virgin as different from all other births. Therefore, it is right and just that the blessed should be called Theotókos and Virgin Mother. For Jesus, who was born of her, was not a mere man.[92]

This incarnate God has rightly come to draw all to Himself, not for His glory but for ours! He is not an egocentric and hungry deity in need of worship, but we are the ones who have been created to benefit from proper worship—we have been made to become partakers of the divine life (cf. 2 Pt 1:4). This is first manifested on the solemnity of the Epiphany when the nations realize that God is now with us. Emmanuel is fulfilling His ancient promise.

Collect for the Mass of the Epiphany

O God, who on this day revealed your Only Begotten Son to the nations by the guidance of a star, grant in your mercy that we, who know you already by faith, may be brought to behold the beauty of your sublime glory. Through our Lord Jesus Christ, your Son, who lives and reigns with you in the unity of the Holy Spirit, God, for ever and ever.

The Gospel for the day is filled not only with the joy of coming to Jesus and the wise men offering their famed gifts of gold, frankincense, and myrrh but also infused with political intrigue and the betrayal so constant in this fallen world.

Of course, this is one of the most iconic scenes of Christmas for all, Christian or not. Here, the wise men come and offer their gifts to the Christ Child and

> when Jesus was born in Bethlehem of Judea, in the days of King Herod, behold, Magi from the east arrived in Jerusalem, saying, "Where is the newborn king of the Jews? We saw his

[92] St. Cyril of Alexandra, *Against Those Who Are Unwilling to Confess that the Holy Virgin is Theotókos* §4, ed., George Dion (Rollinsford, NH: Orthodox Research Center), 11, slightly adjusted.

star at its rising and have come to do him homage." When King Herod heard this, he was greatly troubled, and all Jerusalem with him. Assembling all the chief priests and the scribes of the people, he inquired of them where the Christ was to be born. They said to him, "In Bethlehem of Judea, for thus it has been written through the prophet: And you, Bethlehem, land of Judah, are by no means least among the rulers of Judah; since from you shall come a ruler, who is to shepherd my people Israel."

Then Herod called the magi secretly and ascertained from them the time of the star's appearance. He sent them to Bethlehem and said, "Go and search diligently for the child. When you have found him, bring me word, that I too may go and do him homage." After their audience with the king they set out. And behold, the star that they had seen at its rising preceded them, until it came and stopped over the place where the child was. They were overjoyed at seeing the star, and on entering the house they saw the child with Mary his mother. They prostrated themselves and did him homage. Then they opened their treasures and offered him gifts of gold, frankincense, and myrrh. And having been warned in a dream not to return to Herod, they departed for their country by another way. (Mt 2:1–12)

There is liturgical room after this Gospel for an ancient practice on the solemnity of the Epiphany of the Lord: the announcement of Easter and all the moveable feasts for that year.

Know, dear brethren, that, as we have now, dear brethren (brothers and sisters),

that, as we have rejoiced at the Nativity of our Lord Jesus Christ, so by leave of God's mercy we announce to you also the joy of his Resurrection, who is our Savior.

On the (fill in the date) will fall Ash Wednesday,

and the beginning of the fast of the most sacred Lenten season.

On the (fill in the date) you will celebrate with joy Easter Day, the Paschal feast of our Lord Jesus Christ.

[In those places where the Ascension is observed on Thursday:

(fill in the date) will be the Ascension of our Lord Jesus Christ.]

[In those places where the Ascension is transferred to the Seventh Sunday of Easter:

(fill in the date) will be the Ascension of our Lord Jesus Christ.]

On (fill in the date), feast of Pentecost.

On (fill in the date), the feast of the Most Holy Body and Blood of Christ.

On the (fill in the date), the First Sunday of the Advent of our Lord Jesus Christ,

to whom is honor and glory for ever and ever. Amen.

During this time of Epiphany, let us pray with the Church Fathers on three aspects of this Gospel: first is the end of natural forces controlling our fate, the second is the universality—the catholicity—of Christ's appearance on earth, and then how the gift exchange between the Magi and Baby Jesus results in a new life for those who draw near to the Lord.

First, Church Fathers like St. Gregory of Nazianzus argue that when the star stopped over the scene in Bethlehem, astrology ceased. Why so? "But the stars pursue their own path which Christ the King has assigned to them."[93] At this point, it is a child controlling the constellations and not the stars determining the course of events. Through created goods, God once again invites His people closer. But now His chosen people are not just one race but the entire globe, symbolized by the three Magi. Here, the entire geography of the globe is represented, the Christ Child opening the Father's covenant to all countries and children. This nostalgic event of the three wise men contains great depth for the Church Fathers—it

---

93 Gregory of Nazianzus, *Dogmatic Poem* V.55; the Greek and English translation can be accessed here: https://library.oapen.org/bitstream/handle/20.500.12657/31571/626989.pdf?sequence=1&isAllowed=y.

is the end of magic (and thus the related "Magi," the Greek transliteration of the Persian word for "power" and related to the Persian word for a Zoroastrian priest), it is the gathering of all the nations, and it is a spiritual metaphor for encountering Christ, paying homage, and then redirecting our life's course after such an event.

In his own search for the cause of evil in the world, Augustine came to dismiss astrology as a possible reason some people turned out bad by examining the case of twins. Why is it that twins born under the exact same astrological sign and alignment of all the heavenly bodies can turn out so differently? Augustine confesses:

> Approaching the subject from this aspect and pondering these points, I now turned my attention to the case of twins. I hoped to attack and refute and make a laughing-stock of the demented people who make a living by astrology, and I wanted to make sure that none of them would be in a position to retort that either Firminus (an acquaintance of Augustine's, a fellow rhetor and well-known astrologer, ed.) had lied to me or his father had lied to him. At the birth of twins, then, it usually happens that both are delivered from the womb with only a short interval of time between them; and however great the influence this space of time may be alleged to have in the course of nature, it cannot be measured by human observation and certainly cannot be registered in the charts which an astrologer will later study with a view to making a true forecast. And true it will not be, because anyone who had examined the one same birth horoscope that applied to Esau and Jacob would have been obliged to foretell the same fate for both of them, whereas in fact their destinies were different. The astrologer would therefore have been wrong; or, if he spoke truly and foretold different things for each, he would have done so on the basis of the same data. He could speak the truth only by chance, then, not by skill.[94]

Augustine here refers to the biblical story of the twins Jacob and Esau, whose lives turned out quite differently and for whom

---

94 St. Augustine, *Confessions* 7.6.10; trans. Boulding, *Confessions*, 167.

God had very strong reactions (cf. Rom 9:13), in order to stress that we are free. Unlike many of his pagan counterparts, for whom history was a "sorrowful wheel" of reincarnations and ultimate meaninglessness, Augustine stressed the fact that we could become saints if we only asked God for that grace. Over and over, he preached on forming our desires in line with God's desires for us: we have desires, which shapes our will, and with that will we make choices, and those choices form both our history as well as our eternity.

The *Catechism of the Catholic Church* advises us to think about these serious points when it comes to our natural inclination to worry and the ease we have in turning to the unsavory sources that surround us, offering fake guidance:

> God can reveal the future to his prophets or to other saints. Still, a sound Christian attitude consists in putting oneself confidently into the hands of Providence for whatever concerns the future, and giving up all unhealthy curiosity about it. Improvidence, however, can constitute a lack of responsibility.
>
> All forms of divination are to be rejected: recourse to Satan or demons, conjuring up the dead or other practices falsely supposed to "unveil" the future. Consulting horoscopes, astrology, palm reading, interpretation of omens and lots, the phenomena of clairvoyance, and recourse to mediums all conceal a desire for power over time, history, and, in the last analysis, other human beings, as well as a wish to conciliate hidden powers. They contradict the honor, respect, and loving fear that we owe to God alone.
>
> All practices of magic or sorcery, by which one attempts to tame occult powers, so as to place them at one's service and have a supernatural power over others—even if this were for the sake of restoring their health are gravely contrary to the virtue of religion. These practices are even more to be condemned when accompanied by the intention of harming someone, or when they have recourse to the intervention of demons. Wearing charms is also reprehensible. Spiritism often implies divination or magical practices; the Church for her part warns the

faithful against it. Recourse to so-called traditional cures does not justify either the invocation of evil powers or the exploitation of another's credulity.[95]

Do you check your horoscope? As harmless as that may seem, do you ever wonder if you are showing a lack of trust in God's providence and in your own power of free will?

Do you ever frequent palm readers, tarot card readers, or even dabble in séances or games like the Ouija Board? These practices are "gravely contrary" to your life in Christ, as the *Catechism* states above. Cease immediately.

What "good luck" objects or superstitious practices do you hold on to? Pray over those and see if Jesus is there or see if He is asking you to relinquish those in His name.

The solemnity of the Epiphany also represents the universality of Christ's reign. Whereas the first covenant was focused on a particular people, this new and everlasting covenant is meant for every human—man, woman, and child. Often, the Magi are painted with various skin colors to make this point known. In Armenian Catholicism, the tradition identifies the wise men with names and coun-

95 CCC §2115–17.

try of origin: Caspar of India, Melchior of Persia, and Balthasar of Arabia.

A Carthaginian Christian author named Tertullian (c. 160–240)—very reliable but not technically a Church Father because he split off from the Church to join a pentecostal sect at the end of his life—tells us that the Magi were actually considered great kings of famed territories in the ancient world. These men were inspired by the Holy Spirit to recognize the true kingship of Jesus and thus traveled and emptied their coffers to offer due homage.

> For besides the generally known fact, that the riches of the East, that is to say, its strength and resources, usually consist of gold and spices, it is certainly true of the Creator, that he makes gold the riches of the other nations also. . . . For the East generally regarded the Magi as kings; and Damascus was anciently deemed to belong to Arabia, before it was transferred to Syrophœnicia on the division of the Syria (by Rome). Its riches Christ then received, when he received the tokens thereof in the gold and spices; while the spoils of Samaria were the magi themselves. These having discovered him and honored him with their gifts, and on bended knee adored him as their God and King, through the witness of the star which led their way and guided them, became the spoils of Samaria, that is to say, of idolatry, because, as it is easy enough to see, they believed in Christ. He designated idolatry under the name of Samaria, as that city was shameful for its idolatry. Nor is this an unusual manner for the Creator in his Scriptures to employ names of places figuratively as a metaphor derived from the analogy of their sins. Thus he calls the chief men of the Jews rulers of Sodom, and the nation itself people of Gomorrah. . . . By a similar usage Babylon also in our St. John is a figure of the city of Rome, as being like (Babylon) great and proud in royal power, and warring down the saints of God.[96]

---

96 Tertullian, *Against Marcion*, Bk. 3.13, accessed at https://www.newadvent.org/fathers/03123.htm, slightly adjusted.

Tertullian here collects the sins of the world and represents those locales' leaders as the kings who come to Jesus to atone for those sins through proper worship. One can easily imagine the whole world bowing before the Baby, collectively personified in each of these great leaders.

Over the decades of his pontificate, Pope Leo the Great (440–61) seems to have enjoyed preaching during the Christmas season more than any other time. We still have eight sermons which he had delivered in Rome on the solemnity of the Epiphany (mid-fifth century), always stressing to his people how wide the door to God's love and mercy had become now that the incarnate Son of God identifies with every human. Even though people had fallen into error and superstition, Pope Leo stresses, the providence of God is now working out something new:

> The providential Mercy of God, having determined to succor the perishing world in these latter times, fore-ordained the salvation of all nations in the Person of Christ; in order that, because all nations had long been turned aside from the worship of the true God by wicked error, and even God's peculiar people Israel had nearly entirely fallen away from the enactments of the Law, now that all were shut up under sin, he might have mercy upon all.
>
> For as justice was everywhere failing and the whole world was given over to vanity and wickedness, if the Divine Power had not deferred its judgment, the whole of mankind would have received the sentence of damnation. But wrath was changed to forgiveness, and, that the greatness of the grace to be displayed might be the more conspicuous, it pleased God, to apply the mystery of remission to the abolishing of men's sins at a time when no one could boast of his own merits.
>
> Now when the wise men had worshipped the Lord and finished all their devotions, according to the warning of a dream, they return not by the same route by which they had come. For it compelled them now that they believed in Christ not to walk in the paths of their old line of life, but having entered on a new way to keep away from the errors they had left:

> and it was also to baffle Herod's design, who, under the cloak of homage, was planning a wicked plot against the Infant Jesus. Hence when his crafty hopes were overthrown, the king's wrath rose to a greater fury. For reckoning up the time which the wise men had indicated, he poured out his cruel rage on all the boys of Bethlehem, and in a general massacre of the whole of that city slew the infants, who thus passed to their eternal glory, thinking that, if every single babe was slain there, Christ too would be slain.
>
> But he who was postponing the shedding of his blood for the world's redemption till another time, was carried and brought into Egypt by his parents' aid, and thus sought the ancient cradle of the Hebrew race, and in the power of a greater providence dispensing the princely office of the true Joseph, in that he, the Bread of Life and the Food of reason that came down from heaven, removed that worse than all famines under which the Egyptians' minds were laboring, the lack of truth, nor without that sojourn would the symbolism of that One Victim have been complete; for there first by the slaying of the lamb was fore-shadowed the health-bringing sign of the Cross and the Lord's Passover.[97]

Leo the Great's broad intellect gathers all the mysteries of salvation into this feast day. Like Tertullian, he sees the global nature of sin and even includes Israel in his list of those who have failed to offer God right religion. But in changing his wrath into mercy, God sends us His Son. This, Leo points out, is how God used our wickedness to accomplish His plans, how the weakness of God is greater than any power we think we might wield.

How "universal" is your understanding of the Church? Do you tend to think of Christianity as only a Western or maybe even "suburban" activity once a week on Sunday morning?

[97] Pope Leo the Great, *Sermon* 33.2 and .4 on the Epiphany, New Advent translation: https://www.newadvent.org/fathers/360333.htm, slightly adjusted.

Do you see how detestable Herod's "desire" to see Jesus really is? It is just a pious front to get his own way. Do you ever mask what you really want by appealing to some aspect of Christianity? Or might you sometimes use piety to keep others at a distance?

How do you understand God's providential plan for your life? Do you trust that He is at work and can mold whatever you freely give Him into something beautiful? Do you see how you are neither a determined puppet (with God doing everything and your lacking free will) nor a "lone ranger" (with God doing nothing and just waiting to see what you might offer Him): you are a coworker, a collaborator with the Lord Himself, and all the good you do is a product of His grace, and all the wrong you effect can be remedied and even used if you simply turn back in contrition and receive absolution.

The third major lesson of the Epiphany lies in the gift exchange: as Jesus has come to give the world Himself, it is right and just that we offer Him what it is we are able to bring to the creche. There is an ancient understanding that the Messiah who would save the world would come fulfilling three offices—namely, those of priest, prophet, and king. In fact, this is the way we refer to Jesus Christ in the Rite of Baptism to this day: "The anointing with sacred chrism, perfumed oil consecrated by the bishop, signifies the gift of the Holy Spirit to the newly baptized, who has become a Christian, that is, one 'anointed' by the Holy Spirit, incorporated into Christ who is anointed priest, prophet, and king."[98]

---

98 CCC §1241.

What does one bring a king? Gold. What does one bring a priest? Incense. And what does a prophet receive? Myrrh. While the first two of these gifts are self-explanatory, the third is not. Also, if you studied your readings before Mass today or if you are an especially astute listener, you may have picked up on a discrepancy in the first reading from the prophet today. There you hear:

> Arise! Shine, for your light has come, the glory of the Lord has dawned upon you. Though darkness covers the earth, and thick clouds, the peoples, Upon you the Lord will dawn, and over you his glory will be seen. Nations shall walk by your light, kings by the radiance of your dawning. The Nations Come to Zion; raise your eyes and look about; they all gather and come to you—your sons from afar, your daughters in the arms of their nurses. Then you shall see and be radiant, your heart shall throb and overflow. For the riches of the sea shall be poured out before you, the wealth of nations shall come to you. Caravans of camels shall cover you, dromedaries of Midian and Ephah; all from Sheba shall come bearing gold and frankincense, and heralding the praises of the Lord. (Is 60:1–6)

Did you notice what gift is absent in the Old Testament? Myrrh, an ancient gum-like resin used in the process of embalming a corpse. When we compare the scene of the Magi with Isaiah's prophecy, we see how the true prophet is one prepared to lay his life down for his people.

What could not be envisioned in Judaism is a Messiah who would come to Israel only to die. This would be a defeat no nation could rise above, and what the Jewish people longed for during Jesus's day was a mighty warrior who could free them from Roman rule. But God the Father had a much bigger plan in place: defeating not some dictator but death, gaining for His people not just material comfort but everlasting joys.

In the East, Mary Magdalene is invoked as the "Myrrh Bearer," the faithful woman who courageously comes early to the tomb to assist in the embalming process of Jesus's body. "When the sabbath was over, Mary Magdalene, Mary, the mother of James, and Salome bought spices so that they might go and anoint him" (Mk 16:1). Of course, one of greater means had already started this process, having received permission to take Jesus's dead body down from the cross. "After this, Joseph of Arimathea, secretly a disciple of Jesus for fear of the Jews, asked Pilate if he could remove the body of Jesus. And Pilate permitted it. So he came and took his body. Nicodemus, the one who had first come to him at night, also came bringing a mixture of myrrh and aloes weighing about one hundred pounds" (Jn 19:38–39). Once again, Bethlehem and Golgotha unite, with myrrh being the connection between Jesus's birth and his death. The wood of the cradle is the wood of the cross.

Unlike any other king, the Christ Child is not born in a royal palace but had to beg His way into a stable because no inn would offer Him room. Could this be a metaphor for our own hearts, a perennial invitation to open up more and more and make room for Christ's reign? Unlike any other king, what one sees is not what the whole reality is. One sees a "despised Boy," as Chrysostom will put it, but the reality is truly God lying right before us. How true this is with so many other things—that below the surface the divine is at work and Jesus is beckoning us.

> The Magi rejoiced, because their hopes were not falsified but confirmed, and because the toil of so great travel had not been undertaken in vain. By the mystery of this star they understood that the dignity of the King then born exceeded the measure of all worldly kings. "Mary his mother," not crowned with a diadem or laying on a golden couch; but with barely one garment, not for ornament but for covering, and that such as the wife of a carpenter when abroad might have. Had they therefore come to seek an earthly king, they would have been more confounded than rejoiced, deeming their pains thrown away. But now they looked for a heavenly King; so that though they saw nought of regal state, that star's witness sufficed them, and their eyes rejoiced to behold a despised Boy, the Spirit showing him to their hearts in all his wonderful power, they fell down and worshipped, seeing the man, they acknowledged the God.

> And though it were not then understood what these several gifts mystically signified, that is no difficulty; the same grace that instigated them to the deed, ordained the whole. Let Marcion and Paul of Samosata then blush (heretics who denied the fullness of the incarnation, ed.), who will not see what the Magi saw, those progenitors of the Church adoring God in the flesh. That He was truly in the flesh, the swaddling clothes and the stall prove; yet that they worshipped him not as mere man, but as God, the gifts prove which it was becoming to offer to a God. Let the Jews also be ashamed, seeing the Magi coming before them, and themselves not even earnest to tread in their path.[99]

Try to pray and imagine how Mary might have felt seeing the chest of myrrh open in front of her. Did she sense that the innocent baby she was holding was destined to die for the sins of His people in a such a cruel manner?

This Epiphany, kneel before the crib once again and offer Jesus three gifts of yourself. What could you bring to Him, making a sincere offering of three things in your life you know He wants to hold for and with you.

Remember that every time you genuflect in Church, you are imitating the Magi in their observing Phil 2:10, that before Jesus, "every knee should bend." Do you genuflect in a serious and patient manner, or is it rushed and perfunctory? Does this matter to you? What kind of example are you offering those around you?

---

99 John Chrysostom, *Commentary on Matthew* at 2:11, accessed at https://catenabible.com/mt/2, slightly adjusted.

Traditional Home Blessing: It is customary for the head of the household to lead the family in a house blessing on the solemnity of the Epiphany. Just as the Magi came into the Holy Family's home, we want our houses to be places of Christian integrity, truth, peace, and joy. If possible, have a priest or deacon bless a piece of chalk that can be used to inscribe the sign of the blessing above your home's main entrance.

When all have gathered, a suitable song may be sung.

The leader then makes the Sign of the Cross: "In the Name of the Father, and of the Son . . ."

All reply (R/): "Amen."

The leader greets those present in the following words: "Let us praise God, who fills our hearts and homes with peace. Blessed be God forever."

R/. Blessed be God forever.

Open then with this prayer: "The Word became flesh and made his dwelling place among us. It is Christ who enlightens our hearts and homes with his love. May all who enter this home find Christ's light and love.

Using the blessed chalk, mark the current year and the three initials C+M+B above the main entrance of your home, being sure to place a cross between each of the letters.

It should look something like this:

20+C+M+B+XX

(XX =the last two digits of new year).[100]

After completing the above markings, pray the following prayer: "May all who come to our home this year rejoice to find Christ liv-

---

100 Popular piety has often referred to the CMB here as the three apocryphal names of the three wise men, Caspar, Melchior, and Balthasar. In truth, this is an ancient Latin house blessing: *Christus Mansionem Benedicat*—"May Christ Bless this Home."

ing among us; and may we seek and serve, in everyone we meet, that same Jesus who is Lord of all people, forever and ever. Amen."

If desired, the following intercessions can then be prayed together.

Leader: The Son of God made his home among us. With thanks and praise let us call upon him, with our response, "Stay with us, Lord."

R/. Stay with us, Lord.

Leader: "Lord Jesus Christ, with Mary and Joseph you formed the Holy Family: remain in our home, that we may know you as our guest and honor you as our Head. We pray . . ."

R/. Stay with us, Lord.

Leader: "Lord Jesus Christ, you had no place to lay your head, but in the spirit of poverty accepted the hospitality of your friends: grant that through our help the homeless may obtain proper housing. We pray . . ."

R/. Stay with us, Lord.

Leader: "Lord Jesus Christ, the three kings presented their gifts to you in praise and adoration: grant that those living in this house may use their talents and abilities to your greater glory. We pray . . ."

R/. Stay with us, Lord.

After the intercessions, the leader invites all present to say the Lord's Prayer: "Our Father . . ."

The leader can then say the prayer of blessing with hands folded together in prayer:

Lord God of heaven and earth,
you revealed your only-begotten Son to every nation
by the guidance of a star.
Bless this house and all who inhabit it.
Fill them (us) with the light of Christ,
that their (our) concern for others may reflect your love.
We ask this through Christ our Lord.
R/. Amen.

The leader concludes the rite by signing himself or herself with the Sign of the Cross and saying:

May Christ Jesus dwell with us, keep us from all harm, and make us one in mind and heart, now and forever.

R/. Amen.

It is preferable to end the celebration with a suitable song, for example, "O Come, All Ye Faithful" or "We Three Kings."[101]

Extended Prayer Period

As the Lord's appearance begins to be known more and more—having started with just Mary and the angel Gabriel and now being recognized by worldly leaders from the East—take some time to contemplate the value of both slowness and littleness.

First, the Lord seems to honor the process of gradualness and rarely rushes a desired outcome. He creates in days (see Gn 1) and often heals in stages (e.g., Jn 9). There is something about the slow development of perfection that God somehow wants. He allows our own lives to unfold and does not demand perfection all at once. This should not tempt us toward laxity but should encourage us that, each day on this earth, we have the opportunity to be with Christ and to ask Him to become more and more like Him.

Second, this petition of becoming another Christ does not demand our performing miracles or ascending into heaven later today. It means rejoicing in our humanity, the very means by which God has come to earth and precisely how He meets all of those we read about in the Bible. His eyes and hands, His words and touch, His laughter and His love are open to us as well, and we should not make our discipleship into something stern and severe. The "great things" will be ours, but on God's terms and in His timing, not ours.

---

101 Adapted from the United States Conference of Catholic Bishops, https://www.usccb.org/prayers/blessing-home-and-household-epiphany.

That means that for right now, we simply live our lives as charitably and as evangelically peace filled as possible.

So, as this week draws to a close, pray over Jesus's return to Nazareth and His first pronouncement of the kingdom of God while reading in the local synagogue. There is nothing flashy here, just the presence of a man to whom people are drawn. He makes neither show of fanfare nor promise of comfort and blessing. He simply announces that the kingdom of God is now near. The doubters and naysayers, however, reduce Him just to "the son of Joseph," ignoring how He is obviously somehow different than others they have seen and heard.

> Jesus came to Nazareth, where he had grown up, and went according to his custom into the synagogue on the sabbath day. He stood up to read and was handed a scroll of the prophet Isaiah. He unrolled the scroll and found the passage where it was written: "The Spirit of the Lord is upon me, because he has anointed me to bring glad tidings to the poor. He has sent me to proclaim liberty to captives and recovery of sight to the blind, to let the oppressed go free, and to proclaim a year acceptable to the Lord."
>
> Rolling up the scroll, he handed it back to the attendant and sat down, and the eyes of all in the synagogue looked intently at him. He said to them, "Today this scripture passage is fulfilled in your hearing." And all spoke highly of him and were amazed at the gracious words that came from his mouth. They also asked, "Isn't this the son of Joseph?" (Lk 4:16–22)

Do you tend to think of God only in the grandiose and extraordinary, or do you allow Him to meet you in the slow and the everyday? What might this say about other parts of your life?

Do you understand and appreciate that you, too, have been anointed with the Holy Spirit—both at Baptism and at

Confirmation? You, too, received the same gift Christ refers to in Isaiah above.

What might it mean for you to put this anointing—this strengthening—into practice? How might you proclaim "liberty" to today's "captives," and bring "sight" to the "blind"? Who are today's captive and today's blind?

Week 7

Baptism of the Lord to Candlemas and Ordered Time

Everything the incarnate God does on earth, He does for the salvation of humankind. He need not become flesh, He need not learn human habits and customs, the Son of God need not hunger and thirst, and He certainly never needed to suffer and die ignobly on a cross, counted among common criminals. Everything He does, He does for us. At Jesus's baptism by John in the Jordan, then, we can only begin to fathom His humility, standing in line with those who came to be cleansed from their sins. Did Jesus sin? Of course not. Was Jesus in need of baptism? Of course not. Was Jesus so in love with His fellow man that He chose to share their lot, even if that meant appearing as one in need of the cleansing John's waters offered? Apparently so.

Today, there is rarely any indication that Christmas has been celebrated through February 2 in the past. That day is the feast of Candlemas, which serves as the fortieth day of Christ's birth but also as a foreshadowing of the light He shall bring come Easter. With the reforms of Vatican II, Epiphany became a moveable feast, also determining the date of our celebration of the Lord's Baptism as well. If Epiphany Sunday comes before or on January 6, we celebrate the Baptism of Jesus on the following Sunday. If Epiphany is celebrated on January 7 or 8, Christ's Baptism is then observed on the following Monday, January 8 or 9.

Feast of the Baptism of the Lord

Almighty, ever-living God, who, when Christ had been baptized in the River Jordan and as the Holy Spirit descended upon him, solemnly declared him your beloved Son, grant that your children by adoption, reborn of water and the Holy Spirit, may always be well pleasing to you. Through our Lord Jesus Christ, your Son, who lives and reigns with you in the unity of the Holy Spirit, God, for ever and ever.

This final phase of our retreat begins with the Baptism of the Lord, a fitting opening because this is precisely how your Christian life began as well. The synoptic Gospels all record this pivotal scene—Matthew (as usual) giving the fuller account, with Mark and Luke remembering only the essence of the event.

> Jesus came from Galilee to John at the Jordan to be baptized by him. John tried to prevent him, saying, "I need to be baptized by you, and yet you are coming to me?" Jesus said to him in reply, "Allow it now, for thus it is fitting for us to fulfill all righteousness." Then he allowed him. After Jesus was baptized, he came up from the water and behold, the heavens were opened for him, and he saw the Spirit of God descending like a dove and coming upon him. And a voice came from the heavens, saying, "This is my beloved Son, with whom I am well pleased." (Mt 3:13–17; cf. Mk 1:7–11; Lk 3:21–22)

The Trinity is clearly at work: the Son descends only to rise, the Spirit falls upon Him in power and strength, and the Father clearly confirms that this Son is going to be the mark and measure of all that is pleasing. As with all scenes in Scripture, this is no isolated event but is to be the first of many.

The water of the Jordan is no different than the water of your nearby holy water font. As this retreat comes to a close, stop and thank God for your baptism. He has given you an unmatchable gift, the gift of eternal life, something none of us deserve or could earn. The clearest and most unambiguous answer to why you have been given such a life is, of course, because God is love and God loves you. Yet let's think there is a follow-up point: God has given you great gifts because He wants you to use them in this world, like the waters described by Isaiah:

> Thus says the Lord: Just as from the heavens the rain and snow come down and do not return there till they have watered the earth, making it fertile and fruitful, giving seed to the one who sows and bread to the one who eats, so shall my word be that goes forth from my mouth; it shall not return to me void, but shall do my will, achieving the end for which I sent it. (Is 55:10–11)

When you think about why God has been so good to you, what reason(s) do you give?

Where have you proved responsible with those gifts, and where did you take them for granted?

Have you ever felt that God has disappointed you? Pray over that moment and those feelings, and let Him talk to you there.

When the Church examines the sacrament of Baptism and this moment from the synoptic Gospels of Jesus's coming to the Jordan, we do well to contemplate these three sections from the *Catechism*:

> Jesus' public life begins with his baptism by John in the Jordan. John preaches "a baptism of repentance for the forgiveness of sins" (Lk 3:3). A crowd of sinners—tax collectors and soldiers, Pharisees and Sadducees, and prostitutes—come to be baptized by him. "Then Jesus appears." The Baptist hesitates, but Jesus insists and receives baptism. Then the Holy Spirit, in the form of a dove, comes upon Jesus and a voice from heaven proclaims, "This is my beloved Son" (Mt 3:13–17). This is the manifestation ("Epiphany") of Jesus as Messiah of Israel and Son of God.
>
> The baptism of Jesus is on his part the acceptance and inauguration of his mission as God's suffering Servant. He allows himself to be numbered among sinners; he is already "the Lamb of God, who takes away the sin of the world" (Jn 1:29; cf. Isa 53:12). Already he is anticipating the "baptism" of his bloody death. Already he is coming to "fulfill all righteousness," that is, he is submitting himself entirely to his Father's will: out of love he consents to this baptism of death for the remission of our sins. The Father's voice responds to the Son's acceptance, proclaiming his entire delight in his Son. The Spirit whom Jesus possessed in fullness from his conception comes to "rest on him" (Jn 1:32–33; cf. Is 11:2). Jesus will be the source of the Spirit for all mankind. At his baptism "the heavens were opened" (Mt 3:16)—the heavens that Adam's sin had closed—and the waters were sanctified by the descent of Jesus and the Spirit, a prelude to the new creation.
>
> Through Baptism the Christian is sacramentally assimilated to Jesus, who in his own baptism anticipates his death and resurrection. The Christian must enter into this mystery of humble self-abasement and repentance, go down into the water with Jesus in order to 'rise with him, be reborn of water and the Spirit so as to become the Father's beloved son in the Son and "walk in newness of life" (Rom 6:4). "Let us be buried with Christ by Baptism to rise with him; let us go

> down with him to be raised with him; and let us rise with him to be glorified with him" (St. Gregory of Nazianzus, *Oration* 40.9). "Everything that happened to Christ lets us know that, after the bath of water, the Holy Spirit swoops down upon us from high heaven and that, adopted by the Father's voice, we become sons of God" (St. Hilary of Poitiers, *Commentary on Matthew* 2.5).[102]

In these three sections, the *Catechism* clearly wants to stress Baptism as a mystical death and a rising unto a new life. Is that how your parish describes this rite? Baptism is the beginning of holiness in any person's life, and despite how "cute" the baptized can be and how many photo opportunities such a moment offers, Baptism is ultimately the dying of the fallen self and the resurrection of the Christified self.

The language of the rite makes this clear. For instance, at your Baptism, you too were immersed into Holy Water, and you too were anointed with the Holy Chrism of the Holy Spirit. During that anointing rite, the priest or deacon prayed this prayer over you: "God the Father of our Lord Jesus Christ has freed you from sin, given you a new birth by water and the Holy Spirit, and welcomed you into his holy people. He now anoints you with the chrism of salvation. As Christ was anointed Priest, Prophet, and King, so may you live always as a member of his body, sharing everlasting life."

Sound familiar? There is that trifold office of Jesus Christ now infused into your soul. You too are "priest, prophet, and king." You share in the priesthood of Christ because you too can offer sacrifice—not the Sacrifice of the Mass, of course, but the sacrifice of prayer and fasting, of being charitable when really feeling irked, the sacrifice of honesty and transparency with your spouse and supernatural patience with your children. You share in the prophecy of God when you speak the truth and when you risk that awkward conversation about Jesus and what He is doing in your life. You are a prophet when you speak on behalf of the Lord and invite your

---

102 CCC §535–37.

coworker to a retreat, to Mass, or even to the sacrament of Reconciliation; you are a prophet when you are known for the obvious Christian way of life you lead. You share in the kingship of Christ by reigning over your own senses and life choices. You need no longer be led by animal instinct or brute passion—you have been made sovereign over this world of allure and appeal to order your life in such a way that you are a foretaste of heaven even now.

The Church Fathers, quitting an earthly life to gain a heavenly life, demanded a death of sorts. Baptism offered a symbolic death, being immersed in the water three times just as Jesus was in the tomb for three days. But such a death in Jesus Christ will also lead to new life, symbolized by rising from the water as a new creature, an adopted child of the Father, a coheir with Christ, and a temple of the Holy Spirit. Or, as one early Church manual prayed: "Sanctify this water, that those who are baptized in it may be crucified with Christ, die with him, be buried with him, and rise again through adoption."[103]

> God our Savior planned to recall man from the fall. Man's disobedience separated him from God's household, and God wanted to bring him back. This is why Christ took flesh. . . . Paul surely was an imitator of Christ, and he says, "that I may know him and the power of his resurrection, and may share his sufferings, becoming like him in his death, that if possible I may attain the resurrection from the dead" (Rom 6:5). How can we become like him in his death? By being buried with him in baptism. . . . So also if we are going to change our lives, death must come between what has already happened (ending it) and what is just beginning. How can we accomplish this descent into death? By imitating the burial of Christ through baptism.[104]

---

[103] *Apostolic Constitutions* 7.43; Clément, *The Roots of Christian Mysticism*, 103.

[104] Basil of Caesarea, *On the Holy Spirit* 15; trans. David Anderson, *On the Holy Spirit* (Crestwood, NY: St. Vladimir's Press, 1997), 57–58.

The term Basil and other Greek Fathers use to refer most often to this process of baptismal regeneration is *illumination* or *enlightenment* (this is where the tradition of depicting a saint's head with a bright golden halo comes from). At Baptism, the deifying light of Christ puts to death the old man and infuses the soul with God's own indwelling. Hereafter, the baptized person is never again alone and never again without the grace to transform him or her into a saint.

Have you ever prayerfully looked back at your baptism? Who was there? Who are your godparents? Are there photographs you could pray over?

When you think of yourself as a "priest" offering sacrifice, what comes to mind? Where do you pour out your own body and blood, and toward what end?

When you think of yourself as a "prophet," how do you look to evangelize and become a more and more reliable instrument in the Father's hands?

When you think of yourself as a "king" or "queen," where do you feel you reign best within yourself, and where are you still being defeated when it comes to your interaction with sensible goods and material allurements?

To explain the new life received at Baptism, the later Church developed a category of grace called "operative grace." The word *operative* is essential because, for that split second, the creature had nothing to offer God and so was offered to Him (usually by parents or godparents). God had to go to work on this little one, operate, if you will. Hereafter, however, cooperative grace rules, and now God and the baptized can work together to form a life story that will be full of God's grace and that person's perfection.

At your beginning, God created you good but not yet perfected. This is what the tree in the Garden of Eden represented: that fundamental choice between self and God. In Adam, the entire human race fell, and the integrity that God intended for all the generations to have started from Adam and Eve was ripped apart by their disobedience, our first parents squandering the inheritance that should have been ours.

This is the ugly truth of Christianity—that, "Behold, I was born in guilt, in sin my mother conceived me" (Ps 51:7)—meaning not that sexual intercourse and conception is inherently sinful but that we enter this world short of salvation. We need something more, Someone more.

> But God made you without you. You didn't, after all, give any consent to God's making you. How were you to consent, if you didn't yet exist? So while he made you without you, he doesn't justify you without you. So he made you without your knowing it, he justifies you with your willing consent to it. Yet it's he that does the justifying (in case you should think it's your justice, and go back to the dead losses, the wastage and the muck) for you to be found in him not having your own justice, *which is from the law, but the justice through the faith of Christ, which is from God; justice from faith, to know him and the power of his resurrection, and a share in his sufferings* (Phil 3:9–10). And that will be your power, your strength; a share in Christ's sufferings will be your strength.[105]

---

[105] St. Augustine, *Sermon* 169.13; trans. Edmund Hill, *Sermons (148–183)* (Hyde Rochelle, NY: New City Press, 1992), 231.

Speaking of motherhood and the womb and the vulnerability of unborn life, during this final phase of retreat, January 22 will inevitably fall. This is the sad anniversary of *Roe v. Wade*, which legitimized the taking of innocent human life. The bishops in the United States have asked that this day be a day of prayer and fasting for a greater awareness and protection of the dignity of fragile human life, designating this day as a "Day of Prayer for the Legal Protection of Unborn Children," stating:

> In all the Dioceses of the United States of America, January 22 (or January 23, when January 22 falls on a Sunday) shall be observed as a particular day of prayer for the full restoration of the legal guarantee of the right to life and of penance for violations to the dignity of the human person committed through acts of abortion. The liturgical celebrations for this day may be the "Mass For Giving Thanks to God for the Gift of Human Life" (no. 48/1 of the Masses and Prayers for Various Needs and Occasions), celebrated with white vestments, or the Mass "For the Preservation of Peace and Justice" (no. 30 of the *Masses and Prayers for Various Needs and Occasions*), celebrated with violet vestments.[106]

The Christian soldier being called to take up prayer and fasting to fight some evil is nothing new. We saw how Christmas inaugurated the triduum of martyrs—Stephen, John, and the Holy Innocents—and now we are all called to lay our lives down in whatever way is appropriate so the truth(s) of God can be known.

In an early second-century letter to an otherwise unknown seeker named Diognetus, a Christian author and apologist explained to him the fundamental signs of how Christians live in this fallen world:

> For them, any foreign country is a motherland, and any motherland is a foreign country. Like other men, they marry and

106 *General Instruction on the Roman Missal* §373, "Chapter VIII: Masses and Prayers for Various Needs and Occasions and Masses for the Dead", accessed at: https://www.usccb.org/prayer-and-worship/the-mass/general-instruction-of-the-roman-missal/girm-chapter-8.

> beget children, though they do not expose their infants. Any Christian is free to share his neighbor's table, but never his marriage-bed. Though destiny has placed them here in the flesh, they do not live after the flesh; their days are passed on the earth, but their citizenship is above in the heavens. They obey the prescribed laws, but in their own private lives they transcend the laws. They show love to all men—and all men persecute them. They are misunderstood, and condemned; yet by suffering death they are quickened into life.[107]

Notice what is essential to the second or third generation of Christians. First is the realization that this world is not home. It doesn't matter where one lives on this earth, because this earth is only a stepping-stone into heaven.

Second, marriage and the proper nurturing of human life were key. Monogamy and the caring of the unborn as well as the newborn were a drastic shift from a worldview where women and children were conveniences easily disposed of when useless.

The third characteristic is how real Christians will never really fit into the world's values but will always risk being misunderstood—that although Christians can prove to be the most loyal of citizens, they are nonetheless ridiculed and always viewed as subversive to the common good.

When you look at these three characteristics of early Christians, can you see how you too are called to model these principles?

Do ever gauge your worth by the metrics or optics of this world? As you age, do you see more and more how this world was never meant to be a permanent residence but only a rental property, the condition of which you will have to make account one day?

[107] *Letter to Diognetus* §5; trans. Maxwell Staniforth, *Early Christian Writings: The Apostolic Fathers* (New York: Penguin Classics, 1987), 145.

Do you hold your marriage as your highest vocation and the main way you will grow (or fail) in holiness? Do you seek to grow in prayerful union with your spouse? Are you vulnerable and transparent, desiring holiness together? What might that look like for you?

Do you honor your political officials by praying for them and, if antagonists, not reveling in their demise or laughing at their shortcomings?

In the past, it was more common to keep the symbols and signs of Christmas joy before our eyes throughout the month of January. This was more a private devotion than something in the parishes, but many families would seek to maintain a Christmas spirit until they celebrated Candlemas on February 2, the fortieth day after Christ's birth.

Egeria (sometimes spelled Etheria) was most likely a consecrated woman from Roman Spain who had both great courage and access to great wealth to make a pilgrimage to the Holy Land around 380. Here she chronicled all the significant religious practices and commented on how diverse and deep were the devotions of the peoples here, especially in the great city of Jerusalem. One particular celebration that stuck out to her was Candlemas, as she wrote:

> But certainly the Feast of the Purification is celebrated here with the greatest honour. On this day there is a procession to the Anastasis; all go in procession, and all things are done in order with great joy, just as at Easter. All the priests preach, and also the bishop, always treating of that passage of the Gospel where, on the fortieth day, Joseph and Mary brought the Lord into the Temple, and Simeon and Anna the prophetess, the daughter of Phanuel, saw Him, and of the words which

> they said when they saw the Lord, and of the offerings which the parents presented. And when all things have been celebrated in order as is customary, the sacrament is administered, and so the people are dismissed.[108]

Candlemas, perhaps better known as the Presentation of the Lord, marks the fortieth and final day of Christmas. On this day, it is a tradition in many parts of the world to bring candles to Church to have them blessed and used in a special way for the rest of the year (e.g., your family's "official" prayer candle).

After today, the next time the Church will be illuminated by candles will be at the Easter Vigil, when the deacon enters with only the Paschal candle aflame. As each parishioner reaches over with his or her taper and lights their individual flame, the Church begins to grow aglow with the light of Christ. This extension of light symbolizes perfectly the Advent and Christmas seasons we have been praying with the past few weeks: Christ comes into the world so as to gather a people to Himself and thereby extend His own life through all the world, throughout all time. This is how we too become "a light to the Gentiles and the glory of God's people Israel" (Lk 2:32). This too is why a light shines in the sanctuary of every one of Christ's Churches: God's Light is the Word made flesh, and He dwells with His people forever, His Body and Blood perpetually awaiting and inviting us. Emmanuel—God is with us.

Because Jesus does not want to come to us alone, He builds up this Mystical Body, which is His Church, and the face of that Church is a woman's. Each liturgical season carries with it a Marian hymn, and today marks the transition from the *Alma Redemptoris Mater* to the perhaps better known *Salve Regina*, the Marian hymn for Ordinary Time. The origins of the *Salve Regina* are murky but most often attributed to an eleventh-century Benedictine monk,

---

108 Egeria, *Travels of Egeria*: "The Pilgrimage of Saint Silvia of Aquitania to the Holy Places" (c. 385), trans. "The Pilgrimage of S. Silvia of Aquitania to the Holy Places"; digital.library.upenn.edu. Translated by John H. Bernard. (1896) 385, slightly adjusted.

Hermann of Reichenau. How very Catholic it is to sing each day or night to Our Lady, to thank Mary in song for all she not only did when on earth but also all that she offers through her intercession on our behalf now in heaven.

Salve, Regina, mater misericordiae;
Vita, dulcedo et spes nostra salve.
Ad te clamamus, exsules filii Hevae.
Ad te suspiramus, gementes et flentes
in hac lacrimarum valle.
Eia ergo, advocata nostra,
illos tuos misericordes oculos ad nos converte.
Et Jesum, benedictum fructum ventris tui,
nobis post hoc exsilium ostende.
O clemens, o pia, o dulcis Virgo Maria.

The English is as follows, along with the customary prayer often said at the hymn's conclusion:

Hail, holy Queen, Mother of Mercy,
Hail our life, our sweetness and our hope.
To thee do we cry,
Poor banished children of Eve;
To thee do we send up our sighs,
Mourning and weeping in this valley of tears.
Turn then, most gracious advocate,
Thine eyes of mercy toward us;
And after this our exile,
Show unto us the blessed fruit of thy womb, Jesus.
O clement, O loving,
O sweet Virgin Mary.
V. Pray for us, O holy Mother of God,
R. that we may be made worthy of the promises of Christ.
Let us pray: Almighty, everlasting God, who by the co-operation of the Holy Spirit didst prepare the body and soul of the glorious Virgin-Mother Mary to become a

> dwelling-place meet for thy Son: grant that as we rejoice in her commemoration; so by her fervent intercession we may be delivered from present evils and from everlasting death. Through the same Christ our Lord. Amen.

We yet again are seeing how Christmas engages all the senses. Here, we have the candles for the Presentation offering light and warmth, we have our nightly Marian hymn lifting up our voices and ears into worship, again seeing how the Incarnation has consecrated matter and made all things vehicles for the divine.

> Just as the body of the Lord was glorified when he climbed the mountain and was transfigured into the divine glory and into infinite light, so also the bodies of the saints are glorified and shine like lightning. Just as the interior glory of Christ covered his body and shone completely, in the same way also in the saints the interior power of Christ in them in that day will be poured out externally upon their bodies. For even now at this time they are in their minds participants of his substance and nature. For it is written: "He that sanctifies and the one is sanctified are of one" (Heb 2:11); and: "The glory that you have given me, I have given them" (Jn 17:22). Similarly, as many lamps are lighted from the one, same fire, so also it is necessary that the bodies of the saints, which are members of Christ, become the same which Christ himself is.[109]

Is singing songs with Christian content prayerful for you? Are there any other songs or tunes?

---

109 Pseudo-Macarius, *Fifteenth Homily* §38, trans. George Maloney, *Pseudo-Macarius: The Fifty Spiritual Homilies and the Great Letter* (New York: Paulist Press, 1992), 120–21. "Pseudo-Macarius" is a posthumous label used for an anonymous fifth-century monk whose style was very close to that of Macarius of Egypt (d. 391) and who left behind fifty beautifully crafted spiritual homilies as well as a lengthy missive on how to tame the desires and passions for holiness.

Any thoughts on why singing together is a mainstay of Christianity?

No doubt your parish is filled with candles and votive lights. The faithful often find lighting a candle and offering a prayer very consoling. Do you find candles prayerful? Is there any way you could incorporate this practice at home?

Of course, the celebration of the Presentation begins in the temple when Mary and Joseph, a most religiously and ritually faithful Jewish couple, take their firstborn to Jerusalem and consecrate Him to the Father and to offer the proper sacrifice as a sign of their gratitude for this new life in their arms.

> When the days were completed for their purification according to the law of Moses, Mary and Joseph took Jesus up to Jerusalem to present him to the Lord, just as it is written in the law of the Lord, "Every male that opens the womb shall be consecrated to the Lord, and to offer the sacrifice of a pair of turtledoves or two young pigeons, in accordance with the dictate in the law of the Lord."
>
> Now there was a man in Jerusalem whose name was Simeon. This man was righteous and devout, awaiting the consolation of Israel, and the Holy Spirit was upon him. It had been revealed to him by the Holy Spirit that he should not see death before he had seen the Christ of the Lord. He came in the Spirit into the temple; and when the parents brought in the child Jesus to perform the custom of the law in regard to him, he took him into his arms and blessed God, saying: "Now, Master, you may let your servant go in peace, according to your word, for my eyes have seen your salvation, which you

prepared in the sight of all the peoples: a light for revelation to the Gentiles, and glory for your people Israel."

The child's father and mother were amazed at what was said about him; and Simeon blessed them and said to Mary his mother, "Behold, this child is destined for the fall and rise of many in Israel, and to be a sign that will be contradicted—and you yourself a sword will pierce—so that the thoughts of many hearts may be revealed."

There was also a prophetess, Anna, the daughter of Phanuel, of the tribe of Asher. She was advanced in years, having lived seven years with her husband after her marriage, and then as a widow until she was eighty-four. She never left the temple, but worshiped night and day with fasting and prayer. And coming forward at that very time, she gave thanks to God and spoke about the child to all who were awaiting the redemption of Jerusalem.

When they had fulfilled all the prescriptions of the law of the Lord, they returned to Galilee, to their own town of Nazareth. The child grew and became strong, filled with wisdom; and the favor of God was upon him. (Lk 2:22–40)

The fortieth day after a Jewish boy's birth was a significant milestone (eighty days for a girl). This is first attested to in Leviticus 12, where the author tells us that a mother of a newborn babe is "unclean" or ritually impure. This is not a moral judgment but an earthy awareness that a new mother has been through a physical ordeal and deserves space and time for recovery and rest. Rabbinic sources are quite clear that the "uncleanliness" here is not sin but a wariness around bodily tears and fluids, as well as the intimacy birthing a child demands.

But did Mary need to submit herself to the temple code? Most of the Church Fathers argue "no," in that, having borne from God Himself, without the concupiscence of a man, the Immaculata was exempt from any religious external. But out of humility and example to the community, she went and performed the act of consecration like all the other Jewish mothers.

> So it is evident that the law does not describe as unclean that woman who, without receiving man's seed, gave birth as a virgin. Nor does it so describe the son who was born to her. Nor does it say she had to be cleansed by saving sacrificial offerings. But as our Lord and Savior, who in his divinity was the one who gave that law, when he appeared as a human being, willed to be under the law. . . . So too his Blessed Mother, who by a single privilege was above the law, nevertheless did not shun being made subject to the principles of the law for the sake of showing us an example of humility.[110]

What an intriguing image: Jesus allowed Himself to be baptized by John, although He clearly had no sin to be washed away, because (or, at least, after) He had heard His mother tell the story of her and Joseph going to the temple with Him as a baby, because they wanted to honor God out of humility and not necessity.

> Simeon calls a sword (cf. Lk 2:35) the word that has the power to test and discern thoughts, that penetrates unto the division of soul and spirit, of joints and marrow (cf. Heb 4:12). Indeed ever soul, as the moment of the Passion, underwent a kind of doubt, just as the Lord said: "You will all be scandalized because of me" (Mt 26:31). Therefore Simeon prophesies that Mary herself, while standing by the Cross observing what was happening and hearing what was being said, after the witness of Gabriel, after the secret revelation of the divine conception, after the great showing of miracles, would have known some wavering in her soul. Indeed it was necessary that the Lord should taste death for all and that, having become a sacrificial victim for the world, he would justify all by his blood.
>
> Even you [O Mary], who learned about the Lord from above, will be affected by doubt. This is the sword. "That thoughts out of many hearts may be revealed" (Lk 2:35). This means that, after the scandal caused by the Cross of Christ,

---

110 The Venerable Bede, *Commentary on the Gospels* 1:18, trans. Oden, *Luke: Volume 3 in the Ancient Christian Commentary on Scripture*, 47.

the Lord wished a remedy to follow, both for the disciples and for Mary, confirming their hearts in faith in him.[111]

Basil the Great was very much a practical man, building dioceses and combatting heresies while composing some very important theological treatises. He seems to have been a man who knew human nature very well, and here, in a letter to one who was wondering about the credibility of some Christian claims, Bishop Basil holds up Simeon's sword.

This must have been the essence of a "double-edged" sword, in that it was surely sweet to conceive, birth, caress, and nurture the Son of God who has come to love every one of us into wholeness; yet it was extraordinarily painful to have looked upon those tiny hands and into those precious eyes, sensing that the cruelty of this world would eventually drain the lifeblood from this little body.

Is this "wavering," as Basil writes, a taste of Christ's agony in the garden. Neither Mary nor Jesus are opposed, of course, to the Father's will, but both had to overcome their good and human instincts to make that will happen: as Christ would have to overcome the human desire to live, Mary knew she would have to overcome the maternal desire to hold on to her Son.

Like so many devotions in the Church, the roots are solidly with the Church Fathers, but the blossom only flowers later. In 1232 in Tuscany, seven young men banded together to establish a new religious congregation, the Order of the Servants of Mary—the Servites—fostering devotion to the sorrows of Mary. The traditional number seven eventually became the norm, and Clement IX established a feast for the Seven Sorrows of Mary in 1668. While Pope Innocent XII (d. 1700) renamed it the feast of Our Lady of Sorrows, Pope Pius VII (d. 1823) universalized the feast in 1814, and then Pope Pius X fittingly transferred the feast from a Sunday to an immovable September 15, the day after the Church had (for a much longer time) celebrated the feast of the Holy Cross (September 14

---

111 Basil of Caesarea, *Letter* 260, trans. Luigi Gambero, *Mary and the Church Fathers*, 148.

being the date St. Helena supposedly was shown the real cross on her visit to the Holy Land in 326).

In 1815, Pope Pius VII composed a sort of litany praying over the seven sorrows, the first, of course, being the prophecy of Simeon. After each of the sorrows, a Haily Mary is prayed.

To begin: V. O God, come to my assistance;

R. O Lord, make haste to help me

V. Glory be to the Father, and to the Son, and to the Holy Spirit.

R. As it was in the beginning, is now, and ever shall be, world without end. Amen.

1. The Prophecy of Simeon (Lk 2:34–35)

I grieve for you, O Mary, most sorrowful, in the affliction of your tender heart at the prophecy of the holy and aged Simeon. Dear Mother, by your heart so afflicted, obtain for me the virtue of humility and the gift of the holy fear of God.

Hail Mary . . .

2. The Flight into Egypt (Mt 2:13–21)

I grieve for you, O Mary most sorrowful, in the anguish of your most affectionate heart during the flight into Egypt and your sojourn there. Dear Mother, by your heart so troubled, obtain for me the virtue of generosity, especially toward the poor, and the gift of piety.

Hail Mary . . .

3. The Loss of Jesus for Three Days (Lk 2:41–50)

I grieve for you, O Mary most sorrowful, in those anxieties which tried your troubled heart at the loss of your dear Jesus. Dear Mother, by your heart so full of anguish, obtain for me the virtue of chastity and the gift of knowledge.

Hail Mary . . .

4. The Carrying of the Cross (Jn 19:17)

I grieve for you, O Mary most sorrowful, in the consternation of your heart at meeting Jesus as He carried His cross. Dear Mother, by your heart so troubled, obtain for me the virtue of patience and the gift of fortitude.

Hail Mary . . .

5. The Crucifixion of Jesus (Jn 19:18–30)

I grieve for you, O Mary most sorrowful, in the martyrdom which your generous heart endured in standing near Jesus in His agony. Dear Mother, by your afflicted heart, obtain for me the virtue of temperance and the gift of counsel.

Hail Mary . . .

6. Jesus Taken Down from the Cross (Jn 19:39–40)

I grieve for you, O Mary most sorrowful, in the wounding of your compassionate heart, when the side of Jesus was struck by the lance before His Body was removed from the cross. Dear Mother, by your heart thus transfixed, obtain for me the virtue of fraternal charity and the gift of understanding.

Hail Mary . . .

7. Jesus Laid in the Tomb (Jn 19:39–42)

I grieve for you, O Mary most sorrowful, for the pangs that wrenched your most loving heart at the burial of Jesus. Dear Mother, by your heart sunk in the bitterness of desolation, obtain for me the virtue of diligence and the gift of wisdom.

Hail Mary . . .

Let Us Pray: Let intercession be made for us, we beseech You, O Lord Jesus Christ, now and at the Hour of our death, before the throne of Your mercy, by the Blessed Virgin Mary, Your Mother, whose most holy soul was pierced by a sword of sorrow in the hour of Your bitter Passion. Through You, O Jesus Christ, Savior of the world, Who with the Father and the Holy Spirit lives and reigns world without end. Amen.

As you pray over the seven sorrows of Mary, are there any moments in your life's story that resonate with these? Pray over those moments, uniting those memories with Mary's assurance that the Lord will for sure "lift up the lowly" (Lk 1:52).

Any devotion to St. Joseph is rightly rooted in Matthew 1:19 and Sacred Scripture's inspired assurance that he was a "righteous man." In the Bible, Joseph is a man called to serve quietly: betrothed to Mary (see Mt 1:18–19), guardian of Mary to Bethlehem (see Lk 2:4–7), accompanied her to the Temple to present his foster son Jesus (see Lk 2:22–29), then the man who bravely led Mary and Jesus into Egypt (see Mt 2:13–23) and, finally, he proves a support to her when searching for Jesus in their Passover pilgrimage to the Temple in Jerusalem when Jesus was twelve years old (see Lk 2:41–52). Through all of this, Joseph must have been a humble soul, knowing the Christ Child was not his own biological son and being asked to live in a permanent state of surrender, not sure what the Father might be asking of him at any given moment.

It was in Northern France that explicit devotion to Joseph as husband and father arose, in evidence by the ninth century. This is fairly late, but any Josephine practices of places in the early Church are fairly nonexistent. As devotion increased across Europe, Pope Sixtus IV (1471–84) finally approved the feast of St. Joseph in 1480, still celebrated today on March 19 (the legendary date of

St. Joseph's death). In 1870, Pope Pius IX (1846–78) honored St. Joseph with the title "Patron of the Universal Church," a fitting image given that his entire adult life was spent watching over the Bride and Mother of the Church. As a countering to the Marxist International Workers' Day (popularly known as May Day), which saw human labor only through the lens of class struggle, Pope Pius XII (1939–58) instituted the feast of St. Joseph the Worker on May 1, 1955, in the hope of honoring workers with the dignity and sense of work as honoring God that they deserve.

A St. Joseph prayer arose toward the end of the eighteenth century, which Pope Francis once mentioned was his favorite, challenging the rest of Christendom to recite it and take it to heart:

> Glorious Patriarch St. Joseph, whose power makes the impossible possible, come to my aid in these times of anguish and difficulty.
>
> Take under your protection the serious and troubling situations that I commend to you, that they may have a happy outcome.
>
> My beloved father, all my trust is in you. Let it not be said that I invoked you in vain, and since you can do everything with Jesus and Mary, show me that your goodness is as great as your power.[112]

There is also a traditional prayer many say at the end of their daily Rosary, offering some beautiful images for St. Joseph, as found in the Book of Indulgences:

A partial indulgence is granted to the faithful who invoke St. Joseph, spouse of the Blessed Virgin Mary, with a duly approved prayer (e.g., *Ad te, beate Ioseph*—"To you, Blessed Joseph . . .").

> To you, O blessed Joseph, do we come in our tribulation, and having implored the help of your most holy spouse, we confidently invoke your patronage also. Through that charity which

[112] Pope Francis's General Audience, "Catechesis on St Joseph: 10," on February 2, 2022, accessed here: https://www.vatican.va/content/francesco/en/audiences/2022/documents/20220202-udienza-generale.html.

> bound you to the Immaculate Virgin Mother of God and through the paternal love with which you embraced the Child Jesus, we humbly beg you graciously to regard the inheritance which Jesus Christ has purchased by his Blood, and with your power and strength to aid us in our necessities. O most watchful Guardian of the Holy Family, defend the chosen children of Jesus Christ; O most loving father, ward off from us every contagion of error and corrupting influence; O our most mighty protector, be kind to us and from heaven assist us in our struggle with the power of darkness. As once you rescued the Child Jesus from deadly peril, so now protect God's Holy Church from the snares of the enemy and from all adversity; shield, too, each one of us by your constant protection, so that, supported by your example and your aid, we may be able to live piously, to die in holiness, and to obtain eternal happiness in heaven. Amen.[113]

This last line, "to die in holiness," is precisely where Joseph's patronage lies. Given the fact that he is nowhere near the cross on Good Friday, Church Tradition has always held that Joseph preceded Jesus and Mary in going to heaven, and he has thus been invoked as "Patron of a Happy Death." We again see how birth and death are woven through these Advent and Christmas seasons, and well into the rest of the year. God alone does not come in and out of being, and part of our vocation as baptized Christians is to let God have us wherever we find ourselves on this continuum, from conception to eternal life.

> Think, my dear friends, how the Lord offers us proof after proof that there is going to be a resurrection, of which He has made Jesus Christ the first-fruits by raising Him from the dead. My friends, look how regularly there are processes of resurrection going on at this very moment. The day and the

---

113 *Manual of Indulgences* §19, ed. Apostolic Penitentiary, translated into English from the fourth edition (1999) of *Enchiridion Indulgentiarum: Normae et Concessiones* (Washington, DC: United States Conference of Catholic Bishops), 52–53.

> night show us an example of it; for night sinks to rest, and day arises; day passes away, and night comes again. Or take the fruits of the earth; how, and in what way, does a crop come into being? When the sower goes out and drops each seed into the ground, it falls to the earth shriveled and bare, and decays; but present the power of the Lord's providence raises it from decay, and from that single grain a host of others spring up and yield their fruit.[114]

Like Christ Himself, the Catholic mind sees all of nature offering images and invitations for the kingdom of God, the earth and the sky seeking to tell all of us about the Love that moves the world.

So, as this retreat comes to a close, so does each day. In evidence already by the fourth century, priest and consecrated religious for centuries have ended their day with the "Song of Simeon," which Simeon first spoke to Mary at the scene of the Presentation in the temple. It is perhaps better known as the *Nunc Dimittis*, its opening words in Latin: "Now, Master, you let your servant go in peace. You have fulfilled your promise. My own eyes have seen your salvation, which you have prepared in the sight of all peoples. A light to bring the Gentiles from darkness; the glory of your people Israel" (Lk 2:29–32).

Imagine Simeon and his friend Anna perpetually in the temple, praying and certainly mulling around and getting to know all who came. Don't you, too, have that one or two who seem to always be in Church, sorting the books and bulletins, saying their prayers, smiling at all who are willing to make eye contact? You may even keep your distance from these people, but perhaps they are modern-day Annas and Simeons.

---

114 1 Clement §24, trans. Maxwell Staniforth, *Early Christian Writings*, 33. This letter from Pope Clement (88–99), our fourth pope, was written to the Church in Corinth and stands as one of the earliest extra-biblical texts in all of Christendom.

How do you end each day? Do you have the energy and desire to sit, if for only a minute, and thank God for the blessings of the day and perhaps end with the Song of Simeon?

Are there people in your parish you avoid? Why? Do you at least pray for them and their well-being?

Anna and Simeon are so at home in the Temple, her life story seems to be known by all, and he has no problem approaching a young couple and coaxing their newborn from their arms to hold and caress him.

> The just Simeon saw him with his heart, because he recognized the infant; and he saw him with his eyes, because he took the infant in his arms. Seeing him in both ways, recognizing the Son of God, and cuddling the one begotten of the virgin, he said, *Now, Lord, you are letting your servant go in peace, since my eyes have seen your salvation* (Lk 2:25, 28–30). Notice what he said. You see, he was being kept until he should see with his eyes what he already perceived with faith. He took the baby body, he cradled the body in his arms; on seeing the body, that is on perceiving the Lord in the flesh, he said, *My eyes have seen your salvation*. How do you know that isn't the way in which all flesh is going to see the salvation of God?[115]

A decade or so before the emperor Constantine made Christianity a "licit religion," giving it the same civic rights as the pagan religions, the bishop of Sebaste, in what is today Armenia, Blaise, had been captured by the Roman guards, and they were leading him

[115] St. Augustine, *Sermon* 277.17, trans. Edmund Hill, *Sermons (273–305A)*, (Hyde Park, NY: New City Press), 44.

to his execution. On the way, Bishop Blaise saw a mother trying to dislodge something obstructing her young son's throat. Legend has it that the manly Blaise wrestled himself away from the soldiers and removed the fishbone from the boy's airway. To thank him, the mother and her friends brought candles to Blaise's prison cell for the few days before he was beheaded. This is why, the day after our candles are blessed on the feast of the Presentation, we celebrate the feast (February 3) of St. Blaise and hence receive this blessing at Mass time: "Through the intercession of Saint Blaise, bishop and martyr, may God deliver you from every disease of the throat and from every other illness. In the name of the Father, and of the Son, and of the Holy Spirit."

With this, we now find ourselves back in the green vestments and the liturgical time which, in official terminology, is called "Ordinary Time." Yet, in Church Latin, the term for "Ordinary Time" is *tempus ordinarius*, which we should really translate as "Ordered Time," in that it simply counts the thirty-four weeks (possibly thirty-three) outside the more festal seasons of Advent and Christmas, Lent and Easter. The readings at Mass during these "ordered" weeks are composed in two cycles: an "A, B, and C" cycle for Sundays, and "Year 1 and Year 2" for the weekday readings.

During Year A, the Gospel of Matthew is proclaimed, the Gospel of Mark in Year B, and Year C then takes up the Gospel of Luke, while the Gospel of John is announced during the seasons of Lent and Easter. On Sundays, the first reading is usually from the Old Testament, and then, of course, the Psalm, while the second reading attempts to capture the major themes for that week's Gospel. During the week, the readings alternate between Year 1 readings (read in odd numbered years; e.g., 2025, 2027, etc.) and Year 2 (for even numbered years; e.g., 2024, 2026, etc.), taking us through most of the Old Testament and much of Paul's epistles in the New.

The liturgical color for this time is green, a color traditionally associated with growth and with the virtue of hope. So, in some ways, we are back where we began with the first candle on the Advent wreath—hope. This is fitting because we pilgrims making our way on this earth are in need of a supernatural orientation, empowering us to live in such a way that we never measure our worth by the values of this world, enabling us to realize that we are made for infinitely more than any created good. This is the heart of hope, and this is where we now start our year again. In Dante's usually poetic (and a bit anticlerical) way, the hope that can alone stem from "Eternal Love" outlasts even the most powerful of men:

> No man may be so cursed by priest or pope
> but what the Eternal Love may still return
> hile any thread of green lives on in hope.[116]

As long as one lives on this earth, hope must always reign. There is no time too wasted, no sin too terrible, that the Lord cannot redeem all things. *Dum spiro, spero*—"As long as I breathe, I hope," so goes an ancient adage.

Reflecting on this movement into Ordered Time, the United States Bishops have collectively pronounced: "Ordinary Time is a time for growth and maturation, a time in which the mystery of Christ is called to penetrate ever more deeply into history until all things are finally caught up in Christ. The goal, toward which all of history is directed, is represented by the final Sunday in Ordinary Time, the Solemnity of Our Lord Jesus Christ, King of the Universe."[117]

If Advent and Christmas have taught us anything, it is that God is to be found in the ordinary, in the everyday practice of life, in the art of loving all those in our lives. While it may seem drab, "ordinary" is an awesome term, recognizing that there is an order to things and that the humble will not only recognize such order but do all they can to surrender their life to such direction. The proud, on the other hand, will (mis)use their gift of free will to bend that order to their own whims and fancies. This really is the two types of man—those who recognize they are not the center and determiner of truth against those who have become comfortably com-

---

116 Dante, *The Divine Comedy*: *Purgatorio*, Canto 3.133–35, trans. John Ciardi, *Divine Comedy*, 307.

117 https://www.usccb.org/prayer-worship/liturgical-year/ordinary-time.

placent in thinking they govern what is real and right (simply bring to mind those who today think they have the power to determine what is human life, what constitutes male or female, who should be ordained, and the list goes on and on). Or, as the great C. S. Lewis once commented, "There are only two kinds of people in the end: those who say to God, 'Thy will be done,' and those to whom God says, in the end, 'Thy will be done.'"[118]

So much of what used to be called "normal" has been, in fact, supplanted by those who exert their will over the natural order of things. Accordingly, what used to be considered "natural"—civic justice, sobriety, chastity, patriotism, truth-telling—are now deemed extraordinary and supposedly reserved for a limited number of special folk. Let us never discount the saints by placing them in an elite and reserved category of human. For they are what we too must become. And that is the entire goal of Christmas.

Extended Prayer Period

This final invitation to deeper prayer focuses on the transfiguration of Christ, that unique time on earth where Jesus shows His intimate companions who He truly is, the Son of God. He reveals His divinity when the apostles need it most, on their way to Jerusalem to be with the Lord in His suffering and death. *Lectio Divina* is a very ancient way of sitting with a text and contemplating the scene word by word, image by image, action by action. As you take time to ponder this pivotal moment in the life of the Church, be sure to be intentional on slowing down and stopping and asking Jesus what He might want to show you at any point during this time of your *divine reading*.

> After six days Jesus took Peter, James, and John his brother, and led them up a high mountain by themselves. And he was transfigured before them; his face shone like the sun and his clothes became white as light. And behold, Moses and Elijah

[118] C. S. Lewis (d. 1963), *The Great Divorce*, ch. 9 (New York: HarperOne [1946] 2001), 71.

appeared to them, conversing with him. Then Peter said to Jesus in reply, "Lord, it is good that we are here. If you wish, I will make three tents here, one for you, one for Moses, and one for Elijah."

While he was still speaking, behold, a bright cloud cast a shadow over them, then from the cloud came a voice that said, "This is my beloved Son, with whom I am well pleased; listen to him." When the disciples heard this, they fell prostrate and were very much afraid. But Jesus came and touched them, saying, "Rise, and do not be afraid." And when the disciples raised their eyes, they saw no one else but Jesus alone. (Mt 17:1–8)

Pray over how Peter and the brothers James and John must have felt when being selected to be with Jesus at this moment. Would this lead you to pride or humility that you were asked by name into something very special?

What does "transfiguration" mean for you in your life? Where might Jesus be calling you up a metaphorical mountain to show you a deeper part of Himself? What might you give Him?

Can you let the Father speak to you, "This is my beloved son," "This is my beloved daughter"? Here is the entire heart of the Christian faith and the only key that unlocks our own personal desire for holiness: you are infinitely and perfectly loved; you simply have to allow yourself to be.

Merry Christmas!